A–Z
Family Health
Adviser

A–Z Family Health Adviser

by

'Diocles'

('Diocles' is the pen name of a team of doctors, leading consultants and laymen with special knowledge of medical writing.)

Typeset in 11/12pt Times by County Typesetters, Margate, Kent. Printed and bound in Great Britain by Cox & Wyman Ltd., Reading, Berkshire.

Clarion: published from behind no. 80 Brighton Road, Tadworth, Surrey, England. For information about our company and the other books we publish, visit our web site at www.clarion-books.co.uk

Contents

FOR EMERGENCIES, SEE OVERLEAF

List of Illustrations

EMERGENCY INDEX

Introduction

Men and women are often confused by medical terms. A pain in your back may not seem much until you learn to your horror that you have a 'sub-acute interstitial myositis' and begin to wonder how soon the undertaker will be needed. The pain is no more serious whether it be called backache, lumbago or the title above; but medical terms often give rise to unnecessary alarm. One purpose of this book is to explain the more common medical labels in simple language.

Secondly, there is the question of what you can do, as a layman, about a number of illnesses which may come your way. If in any doubt you must consult your doctor. It takes about six years to train a doctor, and even if this book were twenty times as long it would be impossible to include all the knowledge required to treat even the common illnesses, and more often than not, it is dangerous for the layman to try to do so. But doctors are busy people, and you can help yourself and your doctor considerably by knowing what to do about a number of trivial complaints, what to do in an emergency before the doctor calls, and things you can do when you have to nurse a sick person at home. The main purpose of this book is to answer these questions for you.

Medical knowledge is expanding. Troubles which were incurable years ago can now be treated or helped. Unpleasant old treatments may give place to simpler methods. Surgical operations become ever more effective and safe.

It is important for those with chronic illnesses not to

give up hope. The advance you need may be about to materialise, so keep in touch with your doctor or Medical Centre.

LOOK IN THE INDEX FOR ANY ILLNESS NOT LISTED ALPHABETICALLY AS THE ITEM MAY BE MENTIONED AS PART OF ANOTHER COMPLAINT.

NOTE: Where suitable medicines are mentioned please note that space prevents naming all equivalent preparations which may be equally good. No slur is intended where a particular one which your doctor may prefer happens not to be the example we give.

Healthy Living

Prevention is better than cure. Modern knowledge, especially regarding public health measures, has taught us how to prevent many diseases, and if this knowledge were generally applied to our everyday life the health of the community would be improved. Unfortunately, modern conditions are often in conflict with the ideal of healthy living. Even so, much can be done to assist our bodies to remain healthy, and so give them every chance in any fight against disease.

The human body is an extremely delicate mechanism. To work efficiently it requires a constant supply of fuel, which must be adjusted to the body's needs; it requires regular rest, and it is a prey to many outside influences – attacks by small living organisms, known as germs (bacteria and viruses), excessive heat or cold, violence, unsuitable atmospheres and other factors. Before discussing disease, I shall try to indicate the chief factors in maintaining health. The rules are simple, so simple that they seem hardly worth stating, yet time and again, as a doctor, one sees ill health caused by neglect. Your health is your most precious possession – how precious is often not realised, maybe, until it is almost too late. Guard it.

DIET

Food is the body's fuel, and not only enough but a correct balance between the various types is required to keep the body in health. All foods have a known energy potential usually measured in calories. Broadly speaking, the food we eat can be divided into five categories, which we must look into briefly in order to have some understanding of what is meant by a balanced diet.

a) Carbohydrates

These are sugary and starchy foods whose main purpose is to provide energy for the body. Starches are digested down to sugars before being absorbed into the blood. Sugar is found in sweets, cakes, biscuits, fruit squashes and many tinned and processed foods. Sugar is sometimes called 'empty calories' as it contains no vitamins or trace elements. Starch is present in potatoes, rice, pasta, cereals and bread.

It is now recommended that for healthy eating we should cut down on sugary food but increase the amount of starchy food eaten, especially wholemeal varieties which are high in fibre. The fibre is not absorbed and helps to keep the bowels in good working order and may reduce the incidence of bowel cancer.

b) Fats

Most people are familiar with the various forms such as animal fat, butter, margarine and oils. However, hidden fats occur in such things as biscuits, crisps, peanuts and sausages. Fats are the most highly concentrated form of calories and the foods most important to avoid by anyone wishing to lose weight.

To eat for a healthy heart, avoid animal fats and use oils high in polyunsaturates such as corn oil or sunflower oil. Oily fish is also beneficial.

c) Proteins

The body-building foods. They are vital during the period of growth; and are also necessary in adults to repair and replace body tissues. Proteins are also required to maintain the body's defence against infection, and for the manufacture of substances to deal with invading germs (antibodies). The chief sources of protein in Western diets are meat, fish, poultry, eggs and cheese, although vegetables such as beans contain good protein.

d) Inorganic salts

This term means certain mineral substances which the body needs. Table salt (sodium chloride) is one example. While this is essential for life, it is present in so many foods that most of us eat far more than we need. In some people this may lead to a rise in blood pressure and it is advisable to reduce the amount of salt we add to our food. Calcium is necessary for healthy bones and teeth. Skimmed milk is an excellent source. Iron is needed for the manufacture of red blood cells. This is found in red meats especially liver, egg yolk and green vegetables.

e) Vitamins

These important substances are often misunderstood, being regarded as some kind of 'super tonic' to cure all ills. Vitamins are complex chemical substances, used by the body for certain important functions, but required in only tiny amounts. The body cannot carry on without them and, if they are lacking, serious consequences result. Once the body has sufficient of a particular vitamin it cannot use more. There is thus no point in loading the body with vitamins so long as the basic requirements are present. Some vitamins taken in excess may be harmful. A good mixed diet containing protein (meat, chicken, fish, cheese), milk, bread, cereals, fruit and vegetables will contain all the vitamins needed to remain healthy and they do not need to be considered individually.

In the UK vitamin drops and tablets are available for young children and expectant and nursing mothers at local health clinics.

HEALTHY EATING

For good health, it is important to remain a reasonable

weight. A very large number of people in the UK are overweight and this is the biggest nutritional problem in the Western World. People who are overweight are more likely to develop heart disease, high blood pressure, gall bladder diseases and diabetes.

Unfortunately, some unlucky people do put on weight very easily. There is no magic drug to make people lose weight. Crash dieting rarely produces lasting results. It is far better to aim at a weekly weight loss of 1–2 lbs by eating a diet of 1200–1500 calories per day. This should include protein foods such as lean meat and fish, plenty of fresh fruit and vegetables, wholemeal bread, rice, pasta and potatoes. Fats, sugar and salt should be reduced. Pastry, alcohol and sugar-containing drinks should be avoided.

Once the desired weight is reached, additional calories may be taken but following the same pattern of foods provides a healthy diet for everyone.

Toddlers and children commonly go through a 'food fad' stage. When meat is being refused one of the other protein foods such as milk or eggs can be substituted and these foods can be pleasantly disguised as puddings. Beans are a valuable source of second-class protein and 'baked beans' are usually enjoyed by children.

Mothers worried about the small quantities of 'healthy' foods that their toddlers will eat can usually be reassured that a segment or two of orange, cereal with plenty of milk, a 'disguised' egg and baked beans will satisfy the child's nutritional requirements for the day. The less favoured protein foods should continue to be offered without pressure and gradually they will be accepted. In the meantime no harm is done.

Elderly people who have got into a habit of living on refined bread and margarine, cups of tea and biscuits, need to be encouraged to eat extra fresh vegetables, fruit, fruit juice and oily fish containing vitamin D such as herring, mackerel or salmon. These should be eaten every week particularly in winter when there is little sunshine. Dentures can be a problem and dental advice should be sought if mouth problems are interfering with a reasonable diet.

Pulses such as lentils are a good source of second-class protein and although the soya bean receives more publicity as a protein food than the others it is really just another member of this family.

An increasing number of people are becoming vegetarian. This life style can be very healthy but a wide variety of food is necessary to provide protein, mineral and vitamin requirements. Special books on this subject should be consulted by anyone considering a vegetarian diet.

SLEEP

Sleep is essential, enabling the body to repair the wastages of the day and to replenish energy. People vary in their requirements, but a good working minimum is eight hours for an adult – children need longer, and the elderly need perhaps only five or six hours. Sleeplessness is common, but often due to simple causes. First make sure your bed is comfortable. Expense on a good mattress is well repaid. Bedclothes should be warm but not heavy; in this respect a duvet is useful. Bonuses include easier bedmaking for back sufferers and reduced house dust for asthmatics. The room should be ventilated, never draughty, and as quiet as possible. Try to relax when you go to bed. It is no use taking the worries of the day to bed and expecting sleep. Put your worries aside, make yourself comfortable, and make a conscious effort to relax. For those troubled by sleeplessness, heavy meals and stimulating drinks such as tea or coffee should be avoided at night. Insomnia due to worry can often be cured by getting up, having a biscuit and/or milky drink, and returning to bed more comforted. A long walk late in the evening is a good way of winding down.

(Here a dog comes in handy!)

People require less sleep as they grow older and should not worry if they find that they are sleeping less. Winston Churchill is an example of a man who is said to have taken little sleep but nevertheless achieved great things and lived to a great age. If bereavement or anxieties are making the sleepless hours a misery, see your doctor who may be able to treat the *underlying cause* or prescribe a *mild non-habit forming sedative*. Retired people often like an hour or two's rest after lunch and then stay up later. In some instances worrying over insomnia has a more serious effect than the complaint! See article on INSOMNIA.

EXERCISE

Any machine designed for a particular purpose requires regular use to keep it in good order. The human body is similar, but unfortunately today more and more people use their bodies less and less. Transport takes them to work in the morning; they sit hunched over a desk all day; return home by car or train and collapse into an armchair by the television until bedtime. Is it surprising that under these conditions, their bodies become unhealthy, and a prey to the millions of germs waiting to attack? The energy from food is not required; so, instead of being burnt within the body, a lot of the food is stored up, and the body becomes burdened with increasing quantities of fat. It becomes sluggish so that often a vicious circle is set up. *The less the exercise, the less the inclination to take any and the more flabby and out of condition the body becomes.*

Everyone should aim at some active exercise at least once a day. The city worker could allow extra time on his journey, and walk at least part of the distance to and from work. Advantage should be taken of weekends and holidays to cultivate an out-of-door hobby such as swimming, open air games if fit, or brisk walking. Short jogs, provided the doctor says you are fit, can help.

Walk like a solider, head up, chin and tummy pulled in. The hips, to quote Dr Bill Tucker, a world authority on osteoarthritis, should be kept in the 'pinch-proof' buttock position. The knees should be slightly bent so you use your muscles and not your ligaments. Try sometimes to remember these health-creating points. A bout of exercise should last a few minutes only to begin with and be repeated at five minute intervals in half hour sessions. Choose something you enjoy and your tolerance of the effort involved will soon increase.

FRESH AIR

The same conditions which result in too little exercise tend to limit the use of fresh air. An atmosphere may be unsuitable for the body for several reasons. It may contain injurious impurities; despite the Clean Air Act of 1956, the air in towns still contains toxic matter such as sulphur dioxide and lead (from petrol). The air may be too humid, which means that it carries too much water vapour which interferes with the normal working of the sweat glands. It may contain too little oxygen; normally the body uses up oxygen from the air and releases another gas called carbon dioxide. When a large number of people are in a confined space the oxygen tends to become reduced and the carbon dioxide increases.

The other danger which results from overcrowding and underventilation is the spread of germs. These are always present, but the numbers are enormously increased where people are crowded, so that there is a risk of infectious diseases being spread. Nearly everyone will know how a 'cold', brought into an office by one person, will spread until nearly all the occupants are affected.

Fresh air is highly desirable from many points of view. Most of us cannot choose our work; but we can at least see that windows are open in the office, and in the trains on which we travel *provided draughts and objections from others are avoided!*

Don't become a fanatic, for draughts can harm, but there should be sufficient ventilation to change the room air many times daily without undue commotion. With babies and the over sixty-fives care should be taken to avoid the room temperature dropping below at least 68°–70°F (20°–21°C). These groups are unable to maintain body temperatures easily and are at risk from hypothermia (body damage caused by overcooling). Nevertheless babies need the benefit of circulating air: they should never be tightly swaddled in several layers of blanket.

SMOKING

Smoking is a form of addiction depending on the sedative effect of nicotine on the brain and nervous system. There is no doubt that cigarette smoking is harmful and that it damages lungs, heart, arteries, eyes and digestive system. The lungs become coated with tar causing shortness of breath, bronchitis and worst of all, lung cancer. Smoking is also an important factor in the development of coronary heart disease and blockage of arteries in the legs. Peptic ulcers are more common in smokers and severe defects of vision can occur.

Pipe smoking carries a lower risk, although there is some danger of tongue and lip cancer. Cigars are less harmful and where a cigarette smoker finds that he cannot (will not) break the habit completely, a change to one of these other forms may be useful. Using a low tar brand of cigarette is not a substitute for giving up the habit. See article on ADDICTION.

HOW TO STOP

For those anxious to give up smoking there is no easy road. It is a matter of will-power. The first week without tobacco can be unpleasant, but to cut down gradually only prolongs the agony. The answer is to stop smoking, and to resist the temptation to have 'just one' cigarette.

Some find sucking boiled sweets or chewing gum helps during the early stages. Some people find *nicotine chewing gum*, which your doctor may prescribe (not on the NHS), helpful. After a week or two the urge dies away. It is then easy to do without tobacco provided one is *firm*. Unlike some addictions this one can be abandoned without special treatment because you CAN stop. Having a job where a No Smoking rule applies is useful, as is keeping as busy as possible. Most local health authorities and fund holding practices in the UK run anti-smoking clinics and information about these can be obtained from the Local Community Health Office.

DRINKING

The use of alcohol is widespread in civilised communities. Alcohol is mildly poisonous and therefore the more taken the more injurious it will be. In large quantities over a prolonged period it will cause insidious but permanent damage to the brain, and liver. An occasional social drink is not going to harm or shorten life.

The current recommendation is that men should take not more than 18 drinks per week and women not more than nine where one drink is the equivalent of one *half* pint of beer, one measure of spirits, one glass of table wine or one *small* glass of fortified wine (e.g. sherry). Two or three days every week should be without alcohol. Pregnant women are advised not to take alcohol.

THE BOWELS

The chief function of the bowels is to eliminate waste matter from the body. This is mostly derived from the food we eat, and the waste products of digestion. Usually, plenty of cereal and vegetable fibre and fluids should ensure that the bowels work efficiently. Laxatives which in most instances act by 'flogging' the bowels should be avoided as far as possible. *Any persistent change in bowel habit needs medical investigation.* It is important for health that the bowels should work normally, and it is common under conditions of civilisation to find that they do not. For those who are troubled consult the article on CONSTIPATION.

GENERAL CONSIDERATIONS

Many important items in healthy living have been considered, but it is obvious that these are not all. Stress is a major factor in the modern way of life. The body is largely under the control of the mind, and if this is not in a settled state, the workings of the body can be upset, and ill health a result. It is useless to advise people not to worry. We all have worries, and indeed, life is largely made up of them. The danger lies, not in considering our problems, but in letting them get the upper hand. Don't let your troubles prey on your mind so that you take them to bed with you, re-examine them each morning and finally get into a state where life seems to hold no enjoyment. Keep them under control, and you will find that even serious problems usually develop unexpected turns for the better in time.

If you find that you are constantly ruminating over problems to the detriment of work, sleep or family life, it may be that you need help for an anxiety state. Sometimes talking things over with your spouse or a close friend helps to pinpoint and perhaps reduce the source of stress. If this does not help, you should get your doctor's advice. (*See* ANXIETY STATE.)

Another consideration is one's mental attitude towards health. A man has only one body to last him all his days, and, if it is neglected until past repair, nothing can replace it. The moral is obvious. If you want to remain healthy, do not neglect nature's warnings. Take your body or mind to a doctor for advice as readily as you would take your car to a garage.

It is equally foolish to go to the opposite extreme and imagine that every little ache and pain is a major disorder. The body is a delicate piece of mechanism easily upset. We all suffer from temporary upsets of one kind and another, and these are not of great importance, and soon pass. The conditions for which advice should be sought are too numerous to detail, but in general any departure from the normal which *persists*, or *recurs regularly*, should be a warning sign. Thus an occasional headache attacks nearly all of us, but is without special significance. If, however, you were to wake up with a bad headache *every* morning for a week or ten days without apparent cause you would be foolish not to consult your doctor.

Hypochondriacs are people whose illnesses are largely imaginary and in recent years their numbers seem to have increased; make no mistake, they and their families suffer desperately. This may be due in part to increasing medical information propagated by the media where the emphasis is often on catastrophe rather than hope. We deal more fully with this under MENTAL ILLNESS and other headings later.

Healthy living is not difficult. Beware of cranks and fads; use a liberal dose of common sense in your daily life, exercise moderation (*even in keeping to the rules,* for nothing is more deadly than boredom), and when in doubt consult an expert – your doctor.

A

Abortion (*Miscarriage*)
This term is used when pregnancy ends before the 24th week. After that the condition is known as premature labour. Among lay people the term 'miscarriage' is generally used, as 'abortion' is usually understood to imply an operation, legal or otherwise.

A few women show a little loss of blood when the first period should be due even though they are pregnant. Apart from this there should be no loss or discharge during pregnancy, and if there is it means that something is wrong and a miscarriage is threatened. When this occurs prompt action is needed if the baby is to be saved.

Sometimes during the first three months, often for no apparent reason, the patient begins to lose a little blood. She may also have some low backache, and complain of feeling generally unwell. She should be put to bed immediately, kept warm, and the doctor called urgently. She may go to the toilet but should be in earshot of help and should not lock the door. Any blood or tissue passed should be kept for the doctor's inspection (a chamber pot or child's 'potty' is valuable for this purpose). Internal tampons should be avoided because of the risk of infection. An ordinary sanitary towel is better at this time. Often the blood loss stops quite quickly and after a few days' rest at home the patient may be able to resume normal activities. After a threatened miscarriage or a history of repeated miscarriages it is advisable to abstain from intercourse for the first three months of pregnancy.

If the blood loss continues for more than a few days or if contraction pains develop it is likely that the miscarriage will be inevitable. Your doctor will advise you further and arrange for hospital admission if he feels that this is necessary.

Usually after a miscarriage in hospital the uterus (womb) is gently cleared of any remaining tissue so that blood loss is kept to a minimum. Often a woman is advised to avoid pregnancy for a further two or three months but this is variable and many women are fighting fit within a month.

The abortion law was altered in the UK in 1967 permitting abortion for certain reasons. Termination of pregnancy is now permissible if the physical or mental health of the mother and her existing family is likely to be adversely affected by its continuing to full term. It is also permissible if there is a substantial risk that the infant will be born with a serious malformation or handicap. A declaration to this effect must be signed by two doctors (one of whom must have specialist qualifications in gynaecology) and the operation must be carried out in a clinic or hospital department approved for the purpose by the Department of Health.

An important cause of abnormality in the new-born baby is the occurrence of German measles (rubella) in the mother during the first three months of pregnancy. This is a strong medical indication for termination of pregnancy although of course the mother makes the final choice, bearing in mind the risks.

Your doctor (or the British Pregnancy Advisory Service) will advise you if you need help in this matter.

Abrasion

An injury to the outer skin exposing the deeper layers. These grazes are common, especially in children, and are not serious. The chief danger is infection. Minute living organisms (or germs) may get into the tissues where they cause inflammation and pus or 'festering'.

Abrasions should be cleaned with cooled, boiled water to which some antiseptic has been added. Where clean water is not available saliva which has some 'anti-germ' properties is a useful if crude alternative. ('Suck and spit'.) A small abrasion is best left open to the air to heal. If large, it should be covered with a 'non-stick' dressing (e.g. Melolin) and left for three or four days. If pus develops in spite of this treatment consult your doctor as antibiotics may be needed.

Abscess
A collection of pus. When germs enter the body there is a fight between them and the body's defences, and pus is usually formed. It contains dead germs, dead blood cells and fluid which has poured into the affected area.

Most abscesses are near the surface, due to germs invading the skin and are usually called boils or carbuncles. Sometimes abscesses form internally following various diseases, for instance in the lung after pneumonia. These are serious matters outside our scope. For the treatment of boils and carbuncles see the appropriate headings.

Achilles' Tendon
This is the thick tendon at the back of the ankle which can rupture spontaneously. Pain due to rupture feels like a blow at the back of the calf and the patient can only hobble with difficulty using the flat of the foot. Prompt medical treatment is required (usually surgical repair and/or plaster of Paris).

Acidosis
This term has a precise medical meaning applied to conditions in which the amount of acid in the body, and particularly in the blood, is increased. Often it is used in a wider sense by lay people to cover conditions such as an upset stomach, or vomiting in children. In this sense the condition may be due to excessive eating or

drinking, and is best remedied by giving the stomach a rest. An antacid tablet such as 'Rennies' or 'Milk of Magnesia', and light meals for the rest of the day will usually put matters right.

Acne
A common condition in which the face, and sometimes the upper part of the trunk, is covered with spots. It is caused by blockage of the hair follicle and increased production of sebum or oil whose purpose is to lubricate skin and hair. It is most common in teenagers – and is partly due to glandular changes. Treatment is not easy, but cleanliness – frequent but not excessive washing with medicated or tar soap – helps to reduce the numbers of spots. *Over-enthusiastic cleaning has been found to aggravate the condition in some instances. It is important to avoid squeezing the spots or indeed touching the skin unnecessarily as infection can be spread.*

There are many lotions and creams available from the chemist. These need to be used regularly and do not work instantly. However, if no improvement is seen in three to four weeks go to your doctor who can prescribe additional treatment usually consisting of an antibiotic containing tetracycline or erythromycin. Hair should be kept clean and off the face. Exposure to sunlight may help. Diet appears to play a part in that some patients' skin benefits by a reduction in their carbohydrate intake.

Usually the condition clears up as adult life is reached and the self-conscious teenager should be reassured about this.

The contraceptive pill may aggravate acne and any young woman who has or had acne should bear this in mind when considering contraception.

Acupuncture
Ancient Chinese medical art of inserting fine needles

into specific points on the body determined by the patient's symptoms and pulse information.

It is often used for pain relief and anaesthesia and in the West seems to be of most value in treating chronic pain such as neuralgia and low backache. It has also been used for the treatment of drug addiction.

In China major operations are carried out on the conscious patient using acupuncture as anaesthetic. Relaxants and other drugs may be given at the same time.

Western doctors have no complete explanation for the effects of acupuncture, although as it seems to be of most use in pain relief it is thought possible that it may interfere with the passage of pain sensations through the various nervous junctions. More likely it is due to psychological conditioning of the patient. Acupuncture will not halt any progressive conditions such as cancer and should not be thought of as an alternative treatment in such diseases.

The Chinese deny the psychological story and among other things claim that the needles help to drain harmful forces from the body to restore the natural balance.

Acute
Sudden, short-lived e.g. *acute* appendicitis, which requires immediate treatment. The opposite is 'chronic' which means long, drawn out.

Addiction
An overwhelming desire or need for a drug. This occurs with the 'socially acceptable' drugs (alcohol, nicotine, the benzodiazipan hypnotics and sedatives such as valium) as well as the illegal amphetamines ('speed'), heroin and cocaine ('crack'). Addiction implies that the body has become physically dependent on the drug and that there will be unpleasant withdrawal symptoms if the drug is stopped.

With most drugs (except perhaps nicotine) eventually the addict becomes obsessed with obtaining his supplies at any cost, to the detriment of his work and family life. The final result is total breakdown of mental and physical health unless specialist treatment can be obtained. Even then, cure is difficult and uncertain. *Only a fool would start such bad habits.* There is nothing clever or brave in experimenting with illegal drugs. (*See* DRUG, DRUG ADDICTION *and* SMOKING, *page 16.*)

Adenoids *(Mouth breathing)*

Small patches of tissue which grow at the back of the nose. They are part of the body's defence against germs entering through the nose, and are similar to the tonsils which help to guard against germs entering through the mouth. Sometimes, in children, the adenoids become chronically affected and grow so large as to obstruct nose breathing. When this happens the child speaks with a nasal voice, becomes a mouth-breather, and may have frequent purulent discharge from the nose. This may be associated with recurrent ear infections and hearing difficulty due to passage of the germs along the Eustachian tube to the middle ear (*see Fig. 6 page 102*). It is then necessary to remove the adenoids. This is a small operation and the child should be out of hospital the same day.

If the tonsils are enlarged in such cases they may be removed (*see Fig. 13 page 255*) if thought necessary.

Adrenal Glands

Two small glands situated above the kidneys. They manufacture various substances (hormones) which pass into the blood and help to regulate the workings of the body. One of these, known as *adrenalin*, increases the heart rate and enables the body to act quickly in emergency. Others control many complex bodily functions and are important in coping with stresses such as infection.

After Pains
Pains felt after the birth of the child due to the uterus contracting down to its normal size. (*See* BIRTH.)

AIDS (Acquired Immunodeficiency Syndrome)
This is now the most serious sexually transmitted disease. The first recognised cases were reported in the USA in 1981 in male homosexuals. It is caused by a virus (HIV) which was isolated in 1983. The virus is spread predominantly by sexual intercourse (vaginal and anal) and by infected blood. Whereas spread in the West has been almost entirely amongst homosexuals and drug addicts who share needles, in Africa spread is heterosexual. Many homosexuals have changed their sexual habits but unfortunately heterosexuals are complacent and have not seen the need to do so.

After infection with the HIV virus it remains dormant and only after several years does AIDS develop. It may present with a wide variety of symptoms, ranging from weight loss and diarrhoea to skin cancers or severe chest infection.

At the end of 1994 more than ten million cases of HIV infection had been reported by the World Health Organisation, with a possible million people suffering from AIDS.

There is as yet no cure but current research is producing drugs which slow down progression of the disease.

Air Sickness
(*See* EARACHE, TRAVEL SICKNESS *and* VOMITING.)

Alcoholism
Alcoholic drinks have been consumed for centuries. Research disproves that alcohol is a brain stimulant. It damps the higher functions so that we are less self-conscious, less aware of our shortcomings and generally develop a spirit of goodwill towards others. In excess or

simply taken regularly, alcohol is habit forming. (*See* DRINKING (*page 17*) *and* ADDICTION.) To drink excessively is a sign of weakness not strength.

Damage to the liver can occur long before social effects are obvious. Busy young executives involved in business lunches and trips abroad *are frequently surprised to learn that their liver function tests are abnormal on routine testing.*

At this stage, total abstinence can result in the return of liver functions to normal. If the warning is ignored liver damage can become permanent as cirrhosis develops. This condition may be associated with chronic ill health before jaundice, coma and death eventually supervene.

Alcoholism can be said to exist if the drinking habit is having an adverse effect on the work, family or social life of an individual. Specialist help should be urgently sought as the condition is progressive and disintegration of the personality as well as damage to the brain and other systems of the body can occur. The organisation Alcoholics Anonymous is a great help to most sufferers and its sister organisation Al Anon for the distressed relatives also provides a valuable service.

Delirium tremens (DTs) is a grave condition commonly seen in habitual drinkers. The patient is delirious, trembling and has vivid, unpleasant hallucinations. The condition is so distressing that the patient usually begs for help. Urgent treatment is required, especially if there is accompanying heart failure or pneumonia.

Cheap alcohols such as surgical, industrial and methylated spirits are extremely dangerous as they contain 'wood alcohol' which can cause blindness and death. Tragedies have occurred among young people at parties where punch has been laced with industrial or methylated spirits; such behaviour is criminal.

Other tragedies have resulted from the drinking of large volumes of *spirits* by young men 'for a dare'. Death from acute poisoning can occur quickly in these circumstances. It should not be forgotten that even in modest quantities alcohol is *poison*. It is particularly dangerous if taken with addictive drugs or sedatives, causing coma due to brain damage and/or death due to inhalation of vomit or heart failure.

Allergy

A condition of abnormal sensitivity of the body to certain outside influences. The sensitivity is usually inherited. Some people are allergic to certain foodstuffs e.g. shellfish, nuts, eggs, etc. In those cases there may be puffy swelling of the face or tongue, or skin rash resembling widespread nettle rash. A similar allergic response can occur with antibiotics, notably penicillin.

In some instances, particularly with reactions to insect stings or drugs, the response may be more marked with each attack with sudden breathing distress and collapse.

It is important to note and advise your doctor of any unusual reactions to tablets or proven allergies and to avoid these substances. A bracelet engraved with allergy information and indeed any medical data can be obtained (in the UK) and may be valuable in emergency when for some reason e.g. loss of consciousness, you are unable to give the information verbally.

Whilst avoiding the offending substance is the best treatment for allergy, there are antihistamine drugs available from your chemist or doctor which control it.

Injecting minute doses of suspicious substances into the skin can be a useful way of identifying allergens. The information obtained can be used to make up courses of desensitising vaccines by which regular exposure to gradually increased doses of allergic substances causes reduction of the allergic response. These injections can cause serious reactions and are now only given under specialist supervision in hospital.

Alopecia
(*See* BALDNESS.)

Alzheimer's Disease
A form of dementia, increasingly diagnosed, affecting about twenty-five per cent of persons over 65 with dementia. It is characterised by its relatively early onset in people under 65, and presents with increasing loss of memory and mild confusion. Its cause is still subject to debate and although some treatments have produced limited success for a short time, no real improvement in the prognosis has occurred.

Amenorrhoea
Cessation of normal menstruation – the monthly period in women. Periods normally stop some time between the age of 44 and 54 at the time of the menopause after which the woman is no longer capable of childbearing.

The usual temporary cause of amenorrhoea before this is pregnancy. Many general illnesses, especially if prolonged and debilitating, are associated with absence of the periods, and sometimes a period is missed in a healthy woman for no apparent reason. Worry can also cause amenorrhoea, and a woman may be so worried by the possibility of a pregnancy as to miss a period and thus (so she thinks) confirm her worst fears. A disruption of routine and homesickness can cause missed periods. Nurses, students and female recruits to the forces often suffer from this for the first few months. The contraceptive pill causes light and occasionally missed periods.

In the absence of other symptoms one missed period should not be a cause for alarm, but if a second is missed consult your doctor. Less commonly amenorrhoea may indicate that the ovaries are failing to release eggs in the usual way, and occasionally this occurs in some glandular disorders.

Amenorrhoea is also an important symptom in

anorexia nervosa (*see* ANOREXIA NERVOSA) and indicates that excessive loss of weight has disturbed the girl's hormone balance.

Frequent bouts of amenorrhoea in otherwise healthy young women may be associated with subfertility and such patients should probably avoid the contraceptive pill as ovulation may be so suppressed as to aggravate the subfertility.

Amnesia

Loss of memory. Memory may be lost after head injury and the loss usually covers a variable period before the trauma. In other cases memory loss may be a symptom of mental illness, or stress. The condition calls for expert assessment, but fortunately the memory is usually recovered. Some patients *pretend* to have lost their memories (perhaps to gain attention). (*See* MENTAL ILLNESS.)

Amniocentesis

A test carried out during pregnancy when an abnormality in the unborn baby is suspected. It is carried out by inserting a needle through the abdominal wall and uterus, obtaining a small amount of fluid from the sac (amnion) around the baby.

Anaemia

The average human body contains about eight pints of blood, which is pumped round by the heart and nourishes the tissues. A large part of the blood is composed of small particles known as red blood cells. These carry oxygen from the lungs to all the tissues, and this oxygen is necessary to keep them alive. In anaemia the number of red cells (or corpuscles) is reduced and the body is not able to work as it should. The patient is usually pale since the amount of red pigment in the blood is reduced. Sufferers are easily tired, short of breath, and may have headaches and chest pain. Women suffer more than men since their monthly period causes a drain on the red cells. There are many causes of anaemia, but the most common is shortage of iron in the diet, since iron is required for the manufacture in the body of haemoglobin – the pigment contained in the red cells.

In pregnancy there is even more risk of anaemia developing as enough haemoglobin for two must be obtained. The expectant mother needs extra iron as well as folic acid (another essential factor for developing red cells).

Anaemia may also be due to lack of vitamin B_{12}, vitamin C, thyroid hormone and excessive breakdown or loss of red cells. This last occurs in acute haemorrhage or following frequent small bleeds from 'haemorrhoids' or 'hiatus hernia' (see appropriate headings).

A diet rich in meat, eggs, liver, green vegetables and fresh fruit should correct most mild deficiency states. Supplements of iron and vitamins B and C may help, e.g. ferrous gluconate and multivite tablets each three times a day.

Failure to respond may mean there is a more complex reason for the anaemia and a fuller medical investigation is needed. (*Also see* PERNICIOUS ANAEMIA.)

Anaesthesia
The abolition of pain during operations, usually by putting the patient to sleep. The substance used is called an *anaesthetic* and nitrous oxide (laughing gas) and halothane are probably the best known. They work by damping down the action of the brain until consciousness is lost, and the patient becomes relaxed. Further relaxation is achieved by the use of muscle relaxant injections. Under these conditions operations can be performed painlessly and easily. Anaesthesia is usually induced by an injection into the bloodstream and maintained by gases.

Minor dental operations are usually done under local

anaesthetic. Injections are made into the nerves of the part to be operated on so that no pain can be felt. The dentist's injection into the angle of the jaw is one type of 'nerve block'.

Similar injections can be made around the lower spinal cord rendering the whole of the *lower* half of the body numb. This type of anaesthesia, known as 'epidural', may be used in childbirth. It requires very specialised facilities and not all women wish to have no feeling during such an exciting time.

Many of the benefits of modern surgery are possible only because of the recent improvements in anaes-thetics.

Aneurysm
A weakness in the wall of a blood vessel which causes it to bulge and eventually rupture.

One type may develop in older people in the large blood vessel (aorta) which leaves the heart and can be treated surgically

Another type is found in younger persons in blood vessels to the brain which if ruptured can cause a stroke. These likewise can be treated surgically.

Angina Pectoris
A form of heart disease in which the blood supply to the heart becomess inadequate. As the body ages, the blood vessels, become harder, and thicken so that they are able to carry less blood.

The heart is a muscle which pumps the blood and if the coronary arteries which nourish the heart muscle are hardened the heart cannot work efficiently. When the sufferer attempts something too much for the heart e.g. walking up a hill, a pain (which passes after a short rest) develops in the centre of the chest. Sufferers need medical advice as various medicines may help. Their aim is to open up the circulation in the unaffected arteries and reduce the strain on the heart by slowing it.

The patient can help by giving up smoking, reducing excessive weight, eating a diet low in animal fat and gradually building up physical activity within the limit of his angina. The most suitable exercise to start on is walking on the flat and this may be increased gradually as long as there is no pain.

Many people live for thirty years or more after a diagnosis of angina so never feel discouraged and keep moving!

Anorexia Nervosa

A condition usually in young women who diet excessively sometimes with fatal results. It may be difficult to recognise and treat as these girls are adept at concealing their weight and lack of eating. They are not *always* overweight in the first place and although anorexia means literally loss of appetite, these patients may be controlling a ravenous appetite with will power. Periods of dieting may alternate with 'binges' in which the sufferer gorges secretly and indiscriminately. After a 'binge' the girl may induce vomiting by putting her fingers down her throat. Somewhere along the line the periods stop and this is an important symptom of anorexia.

The condition may represent a failure to come to terms with developing sexuality and the girl often has other symptoms of emotional disturbance. Urgent treatment in a specialist unit is required.

Antibiotics

Powerful drugs obtained originally from living organisms such as yeasts (several can now be synthesised chemically) for treatment of infections. Penicillin was the earliest; others now often used are derivatives of penicillin, tetracycline and erythromycin. The sulphonamides perform a similar function but are not obtained from living tissue and are therefore not strictly speaking anti*biotics*. In the UK these are available on prescription only and the course should always be completed.

Antrum (*Mascilla*)

A hollow in the cheekbone which communicates through a small opening with the nose. The most important hollow spaces in the bones of the skull are the two antra, one in either cheek, and the two sinuses above the eyebrows. Unfortunately, especially after a cold, germs may get into these spaces and set up infection. This results in a chronic discharge from the nose, and pain in the area, a condition known as *sinusitis*. If the antrum is affected there is pain and tenderness in the cheek. If a frontal sinus is affected there is pain above the eyebrows and often a headache on rising which wears off during the day. In this condition the nose must be kept clear to allow the sinus or antrum to drain. Inhalations of the vapour of Friars' Balsam, one teaspoonful to a pint of boiling water are useful. If the condition does not clear quickly your doctor should be consulted.

Anxiety State

Persistent feelings of anxiety such as shaky hands, sweating, palpitations, jumpiness and sleep disturbance. There may be no immediately obvious cause or the sufferer may have long-standing family or work problems with which he can no longer cope. The conditions make it increasingly difficult for the person to solve his problems and medical advice should be sought if talking things over with spouse or close friends does not help. It is *normal* to have anxiety symptoms like shakiness for some hours or days after a severe shock like a narrow escape from a road traffic accident. Thyroid gland troubles can cause these feelings. (*See* GOITRE *and* MENTAL ILLNESS.)

Appendicitis

A disease of civilisation. Food passes from the stomach through a long tube (the intestine) which lies coiled inside the abdomen. At one point there is a small side branch, the *appendix*, which comes to a blind end. (*See Fig. 1.*) In lower animals this is larger and has a part to play in digestion, but in man it is probably only rudimentary.

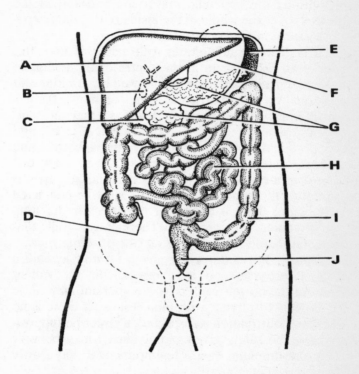

Fig. 1 Contents of the abdominal cavity

A	Liver	F	Stomach
B	Gall bladder	G	Pancreas
C	Duodenum	H	Small intestine
D	Appendix	I	Colon (large intestine)
E	Spleen	J	Rectum

Appendicitis means inflammation of the appendix (all medical terms ending in '-itis' mean inflammation, e.g. cystitis, etc.). Partly-digested food may enter the appendix, and as there are always germs in the intestines, irritation and infection of the appendix may result. This may cause the swelling of the appendix, in the same way as the skin round a boil will swell, so that the infected matter is unable to get out of the blind tube. Appendicitis has then developed, and if allowed to continue the appendix may burst and spread the infection over the whole of the inside of the abdomen – causing peritonitis – a grave condition.

Appendicitis usually starts with a loss of appetite, nausea, an aching pain in the centre of the abdomen around the navel, and may be followed by vomiting and occasionally a little diarrhoea. More commonly there is constipation. There is usually fever, so that the temperature is raised to 99° to 100°F (about 37½°C); and after a while the pain moves down to the right side, and becomes more severe. The patient should be put to bed and a doctor called, as, if it is appendicitis, treatment is to remove the appendix. A doctor must be contacted early before there is danger of the appendix bursting and spreading the infection. There is one rule that everyone should remember. *In a case of stomach ache, particularly in a child, never give a laxative without a doctor's instruction.* If it is appendicitis the violent action of the bowels caused by the aperient may cause the appendix to burst, with fatal results. If there is no fever and constipation is suspected, a glycerine suppository may be safely given. Appendicitis may be very acute and dramatic over a few hours or it may slowly progress over 36 hours.

Arteries
The thick-walled blood vessels which carry blood from the heart. After the blood has been distributed to the tissues of the body it is collected in thin-walled blood

vessels, *the veins*, which return it to the heart. (*See* HEART DISEASE.)

Arteriosclerosis
The condition in which the walls of the arteries become thickened and hard.

Such thickening of the coronary arteries causes angina, whilst arteriosclerosis in the legs causes intermittent calf pain on walking or cold feet. The condition is commonest in smokers, and in those with a tendency to raised blood cholesterol. Smoking should be stopped, and medicines to lower blood cholesterol can be given. A low animal fat diet is probably wise; it has been found that onions, garlic and fish oils are helpful in reducing blood fats, and this may be useful when drugs are poorly tolerated or unavailable.

Arteritis
Inflammation of the wall of an artery. An important type is that which occurs in the scalp temple artery (temporal arteritis) as it may be associated with loss of vision due to the artery to the retina of the eye being permanently damaged. Persistent headache over the temple area in a person (usually) over the age of 65 requires *urgent* medical advice as treatment can preserve vision. Failure to treat may result in sudden blindness – usually in one eye.

Arthritis
Inflammation of the joints, common in the middle-aged and old. There are many varieties. Sometimes one or more joints are affected during some other illness; e.g. German measles. This type of acute arthritis usually clears up completely. (*See* ACUTE.) RHEUMATIC FEVER is also associated with acute inflammation of the joints.

The usual types of arthritis, however, are chronic and develop slowly, and may last for years. The commonest form is OSTEOARTHRITIS which can be thought of as a

37

result of 'wear and tear'. It may also be a late result of injury or fracture. It occurs in the older age groups and commonly in the joints most under stress – such as hips, knees and spine. The joints should remain as mobile as possible and – unless they are acutely inflamed and hot – *exercise is vital. It could be said to be so essential that one's future life and enjoyment depend on it.* Normally 10 minutes a day should suffice. In the large joints such as the hip and knee there is a tendency for the joints to become bent and stiff; exercises aim to straighten these joints to the limit and maintain mobility. Home exercise should avoid going beyond the point of pain. A doctor can outline the exercises needed. A Seton Arthro-Pad can be used for knees, elbows, even ankles, and may bring extraordinary relief. They come in three sizes: small, medium and large. They should only be worn for a few days at a time as regular use of supports weakens muscles. Chemists stock such items.

RHEUMATOID ARTHRITIS affects younger people, more often women. The cause is uncertain although it may be due to altered response to an infection. It starts in the small joints of the hands and wrists and may be associated with general ill health. The joints tend to be more hot and angry than in osteoarthritis.

During the less acute stages sufferers from both these forms of arthritis may be helped by exercise, massage to surrounding muscles, heat or hydrotherapy. Where active exercise is not possible the physiotherapist may put the joint passively through its full range of movement. This is to prevent stiffness and deformity which can develop rapidly in unused joints. All forms of arthritis can benefit from tablets to reduce inflammation and pain, and rheumatoid arthritics may also be treated by injections. Some claim benefits from a course of cod liver oil.

Much relief has been brought to sufferers by replacement of various joints.

Pain relief and better mobility, especially in the hip,

are achieved in an amazingly short space of time and can be performed at almost any age.

Still's disease, a form of Rheumatoid Arthritis in children, requires treatment in a special centre.

Gout is another form of arthritis *(see* GOUT*)*. There are many other types but the general priorities of management are the same. *(See also* BACKACHE *and* EXERCISE, *page 14.)*

Artificial Insemination *(See* INFERTILITY.*)*

Artificial Respiration
This is the technique, more properly known as Rescue Breathing, which allows the rescuer to breathe for a patient who is not breathing for himself. There are two essentials for life – the breathing process to get oxygen into the lungs and bloodstream, and a beating heart to circulate the blood around the body. If breathing or heart beat stops, brain damage will occur within four minutes. The ABC of Resuscitation described below will allow you to deal with any life-threatening situation and provide a means of checking whether the patient needs your help:

A = Approach with caution – Your first concern is for your own safety. Look for dangers such as traffic, electricity, etc. Remember, you will be of no use to the patient if you become injured yourself.

A = Assess consciousness – Assess whether or not the patient is conscious by gently shaking his shoulders and shouting loudly in his ear. If he does not respond, he is unconscious.

A = Assistance – If there is someone else with you, ask them to stay to assist as required. If you are alone, attempt to attract attention by shouting loudly for help. Do not, at this stage, leave the casualty.

A = Airway – The airway is the passageway leading from the mouth and nose down to the lungs and it must remain clear of obstructions – if it becomes blocked,

breathing is impossible and the patient will quickly suf-
focate. The airway of an unconscious patient lying on his
back will be blocked and you must clear it for him. The
cause of the blockage is the tongue, which becomes
floppy during unconsciousness and will obstruct the back
of the airway. To clear the airway, lift the patient's chin
with two fingers and tilt his head slightly (*see Fig. 2a*).
This will clear the tongue from the back of the airway.

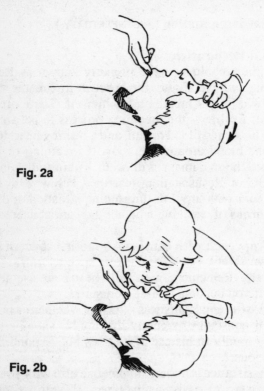

Fig. 2a

Fig. 2b

B = Breathing – To assess whether or not the patient
is breathing, keep the airway clear, put your face close to
his and **look** for chest movement, **listen** for sounds of
breathing and **feel** for breath on the side of your cheek.
Do this for up to ten seconds.

If there is no breathing, you must *immediately* phone for an ambulance. If someone else is there to assist you, send them to make the phone call. (Only if you are totally alone and think the cause of the problem is serious injury or drowning – or if the casualty is a child – should you perform resuscitation for about a minute before going to call an ambulance yourself.) Then give the casualty two Rescue Breaths (see below).

C = Circulation – To assess whether or not the patient has a beating heart you need to check for signs of a circulation. To do this look for any signs of movement (such as swallowing or breathing) and also feel the large pulse running down either side of the neck (the carotid pulse). Feel for the pulse by placing your fingers in the groove between the neck muscle and the Adam's apple. You should do this for no more than ten seconds. If there are no signs of a circulation, or you are at all unsure, assume that the heart has stopped.

If both breathing and circulation are absent, the patient has suffered a **cardiorespiratory arrest** and you will need to perform **cardiopulmonary resuscitation (CPR)** which includes both **Rescue Breathing (artificial respiration) and External Chest Compression (cardiac massage)**. The function of CPR is to buy time before the arrival of an ambulance; it very rarely 'brings people back to life' – which is the reason it is vital to call an ambulance quickly. At this point you should give 15 chest compressions (see below) and continue in cycles of 2 breaths to 15 compressions until the ambulance arrives.

Rescue Breathing (Artificial Respiration) – This is usually given by the 'mouth to mouth' method. Kneel alongside the casualty and make sure the airway is clear and open (remove any visible obstructions, e.g. blood or vomit; lift chin and tilt head). Only remove false teeth if they are very loose or broken. Pinch the patient's nose to close the nostrils (*see Fig. 2b*), take a breath and seal your mouth over his. Breathe steadily into the patient's mouth; you should breathe just hard enough to see the

41

chest rise – this should take about 1½–2 seconds. Remove your mouth, ensure the airway remains clear and allow the victim's chest to fall. Repeat to give two effective rescue breaths in total.

External Chest Compression (Cardiac Massage) – The patient must be lying on his back and on a firm surface – usually the ground. Kneel alongside the patient and find the notch where the ribs join on to the bottom of the breastbone. Place one finger in this notch and one finger on the bony part of the breastbone (if you have small fingers you may need to use two). Place the heel of the other hand alongside the measuring fingers (*see Fig. 2c*). Place the heel of the first hand on top of the other

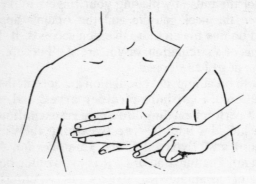

Fig. 2c

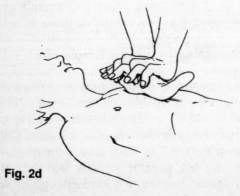

Fig. 2d

and interlock your fingers so that you are only pressing on the breastbone, not the ribs (*see Fig. 2d*). Lock your elbows straight and keep your shoulders directly above your hands while you give 15 chest compressions, at a speed of about 100 a minute (counting aloud 'one, two, three . . .' will ensure you go at the right speed). Each compression should depress the breastbone about 4–5cm (1½–2 inches).

For the patient who is not breathing and has no circulation, give alternate breathing and chest compressions in a ratio of 2 breaths to 15 compressions until the ambulance arrives. You do not need to recheck the breathing or circulation unless there is a sign of life from the patient.

If when you perform your AAAABC checks you find that the patient has stopped breathing, but you are *sure* he still has a circulation, you should do Rescue Breathing only. Give 10 breaths, at your own normal breathing rate – this will take you about one minute. Recheck the circulation. If it is still present, but breathing has not returned, give 10 more breaths. Repeat the process, rechecking the circulation after every 10 breaths.

If the patient does start to breathe again for himself, immediately place him in the RECOVERY POSITION (*see page 222*).

If it is necessary to perform CPR on a child or baby, much less force will be needed. Chest compressions should be done with two fingers on a baby less than one year old and with one hand on a child between one to eight years. Over this age, two hands can be used. Rescue Breathing for children is the same as for adults but with less force. It can be done through the mouth and nose of a baby using just enough breath to make its chest move. The ratio should be 1 breath to 5 compressions on a baby or child under eight. For children over eight, use a ratio of 2 breaths to 15 compressions.

Aspirin
A synthetic drug used all over the world to relieve pain

43

and fever. It is now commonly prescribed by doctors to patients with angina, heart disease or arteriosclerosis to prevent coronary thrombosis or strokes.

It should not be given to children under the age of ten years as it may cause REYE'S SYNDROME (*page 224*).

Asthma

Asthma is a condition of periodic and reversible constriction of the breathing tubes and results in wheezy and difficult breathing. It is often hereditary and may be due to abnormal sensitivity to substances in the environment. (*See* ALLERGY.)

Patients with asthma should be investigated in an attempt to identify their particular sensitivities. The commonest substances causing asthma are pollen, house dust mites and animal fur. The patient may be greatly helped by avoiding the relevant animals; the bedroom, including bed and bedcovers, should be vacuum cleaned daily and bedding should be of synthetic material. The bedroom should be sparsely furnished and clothes kept elsewhere. Mattresses are a major source of house dust and should be sealed in plastic bags. (The house dust mite is a tiny 'insect' invisible to the naked eye.)

Many medicines (tablets and inhalers to open up the breathing tubes) are available to prevent and control attacks. When a severe attack does not improve rapidly on the usual prescribed medicine, a doctor must be contacted as advice and more urgent treatment may be needed (injections, oxygen, etc.). Do not over-use your inhaler in a misguided attempt to avoid troubling your doctor. Failure to gain relief may mean that you need urgent medical reassessment.

All asthmatics should have a peakflow meter, available on NHS prescription, to monitor their asthma.

Moderate exercise and special breathing exercises may help some. Asthma can, however, be made worse by exercise and some sufferers may need to use inhalers containing steroids before playing games, running, etc.

Swimming is a particularly useful activity for asthmatics as it is less likely to provoke breathing constriction and can be used in a graduated training programme which your doctor may outline.

Athlete's Foot
Itchy fungus infection of the skin between the toes; common among the young who take part in swimming and barefoot activities. Avoid public baths and showers until the condition has cleared. Various creams and powders can be bought from a pharmacy. *(See* TINEA.*)*

Autism
A distressing form of learning difficulty in young children. The child is emotionally unresponsive and fails to relate to family and surroundings. This may or may not be associated with other forms of delay in development. Long-term psychiatric treatment in a special centre and advice over management are required.

B

Baby Feeding
(*See* INFANT FEEDING.)

Backache
A common complaint, usually due to a type of muscular rheumatism, or may follow an unaccustomed strain. A hot bath followed by a rub over the affected part with linament will often cure. Overweight, bad posture, and occupations involving much lifting, standing or bending tend to cause backache. Mental stress is also an important cause.

Severe immobilising backache of sudden onset and pain down the leg(s) suggests a slipped disc (*see* SLIPPED DISC) requiring urgent medical advice.

Those with a tendency to recurrent pain should have a hard mattress and put supporting boards under it during acute attacks. Weight loss and attention to general fitness help where appropriate. Exercise during pain-free spells helps to strengthen the muscles in the small of the back. These include lying prone (face downwards) and raising head and shoulders from the ground ten times, followed by raising the legs similarly ten times night and morning.

A supporting corset eases pain but should be reserved for acute episodes as muscles become weak if always supported. In women a chronic low backache is occasionally due to disease or displacement of the womb and in both sexes persistent backache can be a symptom of some internal disorder. If it persists more than a week or two see a doctor, but the majority are not serious and disappear with simple treatment and time. Orthodox investigations of backache often reveal no obvious cause and sufferers are frequently dissatisfied with treatment. Pressure from patients has resulted in various backache groups being formed in the UK and, since the use of CT Scan and NMR (Nuclear Magnetic Resonance) imaging, more precise treatment and diagnosis is forthcoming. (*See* ARTHRITIS, EXERCISE, *page 14 and* OSTEOARTHRITIS.)

Bad Breath
(*See* HALITOSIS.)

Balanitis
Inflammation due to infection under the foreskin in boys and men. Once free, usually by the age of four the foreskin should be fully retracted daily for purposes of washing. In this way the problem should be avoided. (*See* CIRCUMCISION *and* PHIMOSIS.)

Baldness
Loss of hair. Ordinary baldness is almost entirely confined to men and often runs in families. Until recently there was no cure. However, there is a new treatment *(Regaine)* which stimulates new hair growth. It is rubbed into the scalp twice daily and produces a satisfactory growth of hair in about thirty per cent of people. It is very expensive and must be used permanently as if treatment is stopped the hair is lost again. It is more likely to work in younger people who have been bald for less than ten years.

Total loss of scalp and body hair *(Alopecia Totalis)* is an unusual condition occurring in both sexes. In the UK wigs may be supplied by the NHS in cases of total alopecia or where baldness is causing serious mental suffering.

'Hair transplants' can be obtained in a few private clinics. Patches of hair-bearing skin from the back of

47

the neck are transferred to the head – a few at a time –
so the procedure is time-consuming as well as costly.
But it usually works.

Another type affecting both sexes is *Alopecia Areata*
where hair falls out in patches. This may follow a
serious illness, or a lot of worry. In this type of baldness
lost hair always grows again although this takes
months. The process may be speeded by cortisone
applications and treatment for any anxiety.

Bartholin's Glands
Tiny glands on either side of the vaginal opening, they
may become infected or blocked to form a cyst.
Treatment is by a minor operation.

Bed Wetting
(*See* ENURESIS, INCONTINENCE.)

Bee Stings
(*See* STINGS.)

Bell's Palsy
Paralysis of one half of the face usually due to a virus
infection of the nerve which supplies the face muscles.
The face is twisted away from the affected side.
Injection with ACTH (adreno cortico hormone) may
speed recovery but even without treatment the condition usually clears completely in six to eight weeks.

Bends
Occurs in divers who have surfaced too quickly. As
pressure is rapidly reduced, gases bubble out of the
blood causing limb and abdominal pains. Treatment is
recompression in a special decompression chamber as
soon as possible to avoid brain damage.

Bile
Greenish yellow liquid made by the liver and poured

48

into the intestines via the bile duct. It aids digestion in many ways. (*See* GALL BLADDER.)

Biliousness
A lay term describing a temporary digestive upset, particularly nausea and vomiting. *Consult* ACIDOSIS *and* DYSPEPSIA.

Biopsy
Removal of a small piece of tissue for laboratory examination.

Birth
Normally the baby is expelled from the mother's body at about the end of the 40th week of pregnancy. Labour is divided into three stages. The first consists of a dilatation of the neck of the womb, when the regular contractions or 'pains' gradually enlarge the opening until it is big enough for the baby to pass through. The second stage is the gradual descent of the baby from the womb through the female passage (vagina) until it leaves the mother's body. In the third stage the womb contracts in size and finally expels the placenta, or afterbirth. This is a large mass of tissue attached to the inside of the womb from which the baby draws nourishment from the mother.

Normally the patient should be under the care of a doctor or midwife. It sometimes happens that a birth occurs in some out-of-the-way place or starts early and unexpectedly before medical aid can be summoned. Under these circumstances a lay person may have to help the mother. Labour is usually heralded by a show of mucus (slime) and blood or sometimes by 'the waters' breaking. Successive labours tend to be shorter by several hours and anyone with a history of a previously rapid labour should make allowances for this. If the previous birth was extremely quick it is often wisest for an arrangement to be made whereby the mother is taken into hospital a week prior to the expected delivery date.

When the contraction pains last more than half a minute and occur at regular intervals of fifteen to twenty minutes it means that the first stage of labour is under way. At this point (or if the waters break) the patient is advised to enter hospital or contact the doctor. If this help is delayed, a warm bedroom should be prepared and the bed made with freshly laundered linen. The mother may lie on her side or back. At the end of the first stage, contractions occur roughly every three minutes or so and last for about one and a half minutes. When the second stage begins, the mother usually has a strong desire to bear down and can be encouraged to do so. When the baby's head appears it should be restrained for a little by pressure from the well-washed hand of the person helping. At this point the mother should be asked to pant and not push. This is to prevent *sudden* stretching of the external parts which might get torn.

After the head is born, the rest of the body normally follows quickly and easily. The baby will still be attached to the mother by the umbilical cord, and this should be tied in two places, an inch or two apart, with clean thread six inches away from the baby. It should then be cut *between the threads* with clean (preferably boiled) scissors, which will prevent bleeding from the cord. There is no hurry about this cord cutting: if suitable implements are not available the afterbirth can be delivered whilst still attached to the cord; indeed leave well alone if medical help is expected within an hour or less. The important thing is to check on the condition of the baby and mother. If bleeding is excessive, treat as below. *If no medical help is forthcoming that day* and the above implements are not to hand, the cord can be tied with fine clean string and cut with a clean sharp knife (even teeth in emergency). The baby may be smacked once or twice if he does not breathe or cry within twenty seconds of the birth and then should be wrapped in warm clothing and left in peace. If there is no response to smacking, *gentle* mouth to mouth breathing should be used until medical help arrives (*see* ARTIFICIAL RESPIRATION). Mucus may be cleared from the baby's nose and mouth by suction through any available tubing or drinking straw.

The mother should be covered in warm bedclothes, and she will probably produce the 'afterbirth' in a short while. If the afterbirth is not delivered within an hour or so, the patient is in danger from excessive bleeding. If there *is* considerable bleeding after the baby is born, raise the foot of the bed (e.g. on a chair) so that the mother's head is lower than her buttocks. She should be kept especially warm. In the event of such haemorrhage, *in remote areas where medical help is not available,* firm downwards pressure of the hand on the stomach above the uterus (felt as a firm muscular swelling just below the navel) should expel the afterbirth. If bleeding continues, the uterus (womb) can be squeezed firmly by a hand placed on the abdomen above, when usually the womb will contract to stop the blood loss. The afterbirth should be saved for the doctor's inspection so that he may see if it is complete. *No unqualified person should attempt to conduct a birth unless there is no alternative, and every effort must be made to get a doctor, midwife or nurse at the earliest.* Apart from haemorrhage the birth outlined above is a normal one. *It must be again stressed that births can go wrong very suddenly and it would be a very grave matter if every attempt had not been made to get medical aid quickly.*

More complicated births such as breech deliveries (buttocks first) and forceps deliveries can occur, which are outside our scope. Under modern conditions the mother experiences very little more discomfort than with a normal birth (local or general anaesthetic may be used) and the assisted delivery may be life saving.

Natural Childbirth

It is no longer felt that natural childbirth can be completely painless, and any mother who feels the need for pain relief should request this. Knowledge about pregnancy and labour and some form of relaxation exercises help the woman to cope with labour and need the minimum amount of painkillers and sedatives. *In the normal birth, the less afraid the woman is, the less will be her pain.*

Grantly Dick-Read was one of the pioneers of natural childbirth who thought that by overcoming fear and by reducing ignorance with knowledge, women could have a 'natural', relatively painless birth. Many modifications of his ideas followed. At present in the UK most women are taught a modified version of psychoprophylaxis plus general relaxation. The aim is to 'distract' the woman from the pain of the contractions by training her to *concentrate* on tightening other muscles or performing breathing exercises. This, together with the support of her husband who can be a useful companion during the first stage, can lead to a comfortable labour. It does not guarantee a *normal* labour; complications may still arise and the mother should not feel that this is due to any failure on her part. The National Childbirth Trust advises women on all matters relating to pregnancy, psychoprophylaxis and birth.

At the other end of the spectrum from childbirth with the minimum of drugs is a trend towards epidural anaesthesia (*see* ANAESTHESIA). Ideally, the mother can spend the whole labour free of pain. Here, the forceps delivery percentage tends to be higher as there is little urge to push in the second stage.

Caesarian Operation

The operation by which a living child is taken from the mother's womb by an incision through the abdomen. The name is derived from Roman times. Caesarian section is not particularly difficult and can be used in cases where normal birth might be hazardous. It should have no serious after-effects, and many patients consider it less unpleasant than normal labour. A Caesarian section is no bar to having subsequent children. The scar can usually be hidden by a bikini! After a Caesarian the mother takes a little longer to find her feet but all the advice below applies.

Most mothers feel low a few days after delivery – 'fourth day blues'. This should disappear a week or so later, and a mother feeling seriously depressed after the first ten days should see the doctor urgently as post-natal depression can be severe, but responds well to prompt treatment.

There is a lot of tiredness in the early weeks after a baby, as demands are great and sleep disturbed. Mothers should take as much rest as possible between the demands of the infant and take advantage (without guilt) of offers of help from fond relatives or friends. Apart from establishing a routine for the baby, this is not the time to get obsessional about housework. Aim to get out with your husband at least once a week!

Mothers should take extra iron for a few weeks after delivery to replenish iron stores. They should be sure to attend for post-natal examination six weeks after delivery to check that all is well and for contraceptive advice.

Birth Control
(*See* CONTRACEPTION.)

Birthmark (*Naevus*)
There are several types of mark which may be apparent on the skin at birth. The 'port wine' stain varies from pink to dark bluish red and unfortunately often occurs on the face. Surgical treatment is disappointing. There are however some excellent creams such as 'Cover-mark' and 'Keromask' which can be bought or obtained

on doctor's prescription in severe cases.

The 'strawberry mark' is quite a common naevus. It may be inconspicuous at birth and then, to the distress of the baby's parents, often grows alarmingly in size and thickness in the early months, becoming purple in colour. In spite of this, the outlook is excellent as after growing for perhaps as long as two or three years it normally disappears by the age of four to seven. Usually no treatment is needed. Parents can be reassured that a strawberry mark or 'cavernous haemangioma' will always get smaller in the long run. They should not think they are being fobbed off by a busy doctor when he reassures them on this. The only indication for operation is when there is recurrent bleeding due to friction from clothing, etc.

The tiny pale pink marks on the eyelids and back of the neck in about fifty per cent of babies fade naturally and are nothing to worry about.

Blackheads (*See also* ACNE.)
Small black spots in the skin due to a collection of debris in the openings of the hair follicles. The general treatment for ACNE and blackheads is the same, and the two conditions are commonly found together.

Bleeding
(*See* HAEMORRHAGE *and* BIRTH.)

Blood Groups
Blood can be divided into four main groups – A, B, O and AB. These depend on the presence or absence of antibodies which will attack and break down the red cells of a different group, e.g. if blood group A is given to a patient of group O, the antibodies of the patient destroy the transfused red cells causing severe illness with shaking and fever.

The A, B, O groups can be further sub-divided into rhesus positive and rhesus negative (*see* RHESUS FACTOR).

All patients must receive the correct ABO and rhesus group blood for successful transfusion.

Patients often wish to know their blood group. The best way to find out is to enrol as a blood donor. You will be tested immediately. In disputed paternity, blood groups can sometimes be used to prove that a man is *not* the father; they can never prove that he is.

Blood Pressure

The heart is a specially adapted muscle which pumps blood through blood vessels around the body. This results in the blood being under pressure, and since the vessels become hardened with age, and have less 'give', the blood pressure tends to rise. It is thus *normal* to have a rather higher blood pressure at sixty than at twenty. At an earlier age in certain conditions, kidney disease, gland disease, and sometimes for no apparent reason, the pressure may rise to dangerous levels. The chief risks are that the heart may be unable to cope or a blood vessel may burst in some organ such as the brain (*see* STROKE).

Even in normal persons the pressure varies greatly and there is a wide margin of increased pressure that the heart and vessels can deal with without great danger. Lay people tend to be frightened of hypertension, but those with a moderate rise in the pressure may live for years. Many sufferers have reached great age, and died from something unconnected. Be advised by your doctor. He will probably arrange tests to see if there is a curable cause and check for any sign of adverse effect on heart or kidneys. He will suggest a reducing diet if you are overweight, abstention from smoking and reduction of animal fats and salt. He may perhaps prescribe tablets to reduce the pressure. There are usually no symptoms of raised blood pressure; it is often found during a routine medical insurance examination. Occasionally, headaches and giddiness are found to be caused by raised blood pressure. Once you are known to have raised blood pressure you will need the pressure checked occasionally (be guided by your own doctor), as treatment may need to be adjusted. You should continue accustomed activities but if you have taken no exercise for years do not suddenly take up vigorous exercise such as squash; start gradually with short walks and build up.

Blood Tests
Many conditions can be checked on by blood tests. Anaemia and other blood diseases can be detected as can kidney and liver disorders and some venereal diseases. Too much cholesterol (a fatty substance associated with heart and artery disease) may be found and many chronic illnesses, glandular diseases and forms of arthritis can be confirmed by blood tests. The blood levels of alcohol, drugs and poisons may be measured (it is sometimes useful to know if the patient is taking his tablets!). One value of tests is that, if negative, they reassure the patient who may be fearing the worst. (*See* BLOOD GROUPS.)

Blood Transfusion
This technique of transferring blood from a healthy donor to a patient saves many lives. Operations, once impossible, can be performed with relative safety, and accident cases, perhaps bleeding after childbirth, have a better chance of recovery, as have some kinds of anaemia; 'Blood banks' are kept to be readily available in emergency, and giving blood for transfusion is safe, and simple. Everyone who is healthy and not in a risk group for AIDS should volunteer. (*See* BLOOD GROUPS *and* AIDS.)

Blue Baby
Person born with one or more heart defects hindering the blood being pumped efficiently to the lungs. This results in blood lacking oxygen being sent to the rest of

the body so that the patient looks blue or dusky. Good results are now obtained by surgery. Patients with this history have had normal babies after an uncomplicated pregnancy and birth.

Boils

Abscesses develop in the skin due to infection by germs. These usually enter through small openings of the sweat glands. The best home remedy is to apply Anaflex powder spray and cover with a non-stick (Melolin) dressing. Do not squeeze. If it does not clear or if boils appear in crops, consult your doctor. Attention to cleanliness, particularly of the hands, plus a balanced diet should keep boils to a minimum. A sufferer should keep to his own towels and facecloths which should be boiled after use. Disposable tissues and towels are even safer. (*See* ABSCESS.)

Bone Infection

(*See* OSTEOMYELITIS.)

Brain and Body Scanners *(Scan)*

A British invention using computer assisted X-rays to scan the brain and the rest of the body. The resulting pictures show details of structures deep in the brain or body and can help detect many diseases early.

Breast

A normally inactive gland which after a birth begins to function and produce milk (lactation). Sometimes perseverance is needed before breast feeding is established, and a mother should try because breast milk is best for the infant. It contains valuable substances for warding off infection which cannot be replaced artificially. *Where there is a family history of allergy (asthma and eczema), breast feeding may protect the baby against later allergic illness*. It should be continued for as long as possible, perhaps up to nine months, although of course other solids may be introduced at four to six months. Sometimes during lactation germs enter the breast, which becomes painful and inflamed, and a breast abscess (*see* ABSCESS) may develop. This is usually preceded by a sore, cracked nipple; modern sprays and careful drying after washing with plain water should prevent this condition but if it does occur seek medical advice at the onset so that abscess formation is prevented. Antibiotics can cure at this stage and breast feeding continue. If an abscess does develop, hot poultices may be applied as an emergency, but urgent medical advice is required.

Any lump in the breast, or problem, at any age, calls for medical advice.

Self-examination of the breasts
Examine your breasts regularly, at the same time each month, e.g. the day after your period ceases or if you have passed the 'change of life', the first day of the calendar month.

Examine the upper part of the breast, including the armpit, then the lower and central parts of the breast.

With your right hand, examine the whole of your left breast, as shown in the diagrams, starting at the armpit. Then examine the right breast with the left hand. Follow the sequence shown in Fig. 3, nos. 1 to 4.

It is important to use the flat of your hand, keeping your finger tips held lightly together, making sure that the finger tips, the most sensitive part of the hand, follow the same path as the flat of your hand.

Should you find a lump in the breast, or any of the following 'warning signs', which was not present last month, go to your doctor and say 'I have a lump in my breast' or 'There is something wrong which I was not aware of last month'.

Tell him carefully what difference you have noticed, and ask his advice. Through lack of knowledge some women only report to their doctor when a lump or

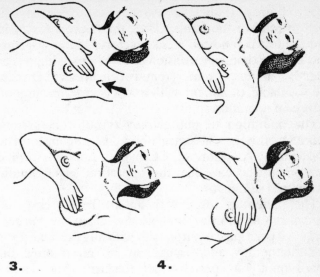

Fig. 3 Self examination of the breasts

swelling in the breast has been present a long time. The following points may be 'warning signs' that something could be wrong:

1. A lump or swelling in the breast.
2. Pain in the breast, not confined to the time just before a period.
3. A stained discharge from the nipple, or skin trouble around the nipple, or a 'pulling in' of the nipple.
4. An alteration in the appearance of the breast, e.g. dimpling or puckering of the skin.
5. A change in shape or size of one breast, compared with the other breast, which has occurred during the month.

Most of the above symptoms require specialist

investigation. Tests include special X-rays or mammography; drawing off fluid if it is a cystic swelling or needle biopsy. If there is a doubt, the specialist will wish to remove the lump. Often the lump is removed and the test is reported as satisfactory. Many surgeons now believe that wide excision of a malignant lump is as effective as mastectomy (removal of breast). Discuss the available treatment with your doctor or surgeon before an operation.

The operation of mastectomy is not very serious although the psychological blow is immense. The Mastectomy Association, of Croydon, London, formed by women who have had this operation, gives general advice and support.

The patient is fitted with an artificial breast and special bra as soon as possible and again the Mastectomy Association can often help with any problems.

Radiotherapy and drugs may be given after the operation if your specialist feels this necessary. Careful follow-up is needed and the patient should never lose touch with her specialist unless discharged. The outlook can be good if the lump is caught early. Many sprightly eighty-year-olds had successful operations thirty years ago.

Information on self-examination of the breasts courtesy of South-West Thames Regional Cancer Services.

Breast Screening
A national programme introduced by the NHS consisting of mammography and breast examination in women over 45.

Bronchiectasis
A chronic lung infection due to weakness and distortion of the smaller breathing tubes or bronchi. It can sometimes be helped by an operation to remove the affected part of the lung. It can be an after-effect of

whooping cough and is one good reason for having infants immunised in the first year of life.

Bronchiolitis
A severe infection of the smallest breathing tubes in babies. Any baby with breathing difficulty needs urgent medical attention. A humid warm atmosphere helps temporarily. (*See* CROUP.)

Bronchitis
A common complaint, especially in winter, and often follows a 'cold'. Smokers and workers in dusty, polluted atmospheres are most affected. In infants bronchitis tends to be a recurrent problem.

It may not at first be noticeable except for a morning cough, but after the additional insult of a virus infection the lining of the breathing tubes becomes swollen and inflamed. There is often pain in the chest, raised temperature, cough, and the production of sputum. The patient is best in bed in a warm atmosphere. Lemon and honey mixtures are soothing and, if there is fever, aspirin or paracetamol is indicated. Inhalation of Friars' Balsam is a well tried remedy, but medical advice is needed as antibiotics may be required. Stop smoking for good, as this illness tends to recur if the bronchi are repeatedly irritated. The end result of repeated attacks can be extreme shortness of breath even at rest, and this must be avoided. (*See* SMOKING, page 16.)

Apart from stopping smoking ask your doctor's advice about anti-flu injections in the autumn and let him know when you have a minor cold. He may wish you to start antibiotics at the first sign. (This does not apply to the vast majority of 'healthy' folk who should rarely need antibiotics.) Stay in bed with bronchitis since there is a danger of pneumonia. Keep your legs moving while on bedrest. Do not go outdoors until fit.

Broncho-pneumonia

A type of pneumonia in which the infection spreads from the breathing tubes, or bronchi, into the lung substance. (*See* PNEUMONIA.)

Bronchoscopy

A procedure whereby the specialist uses an illuminated tube to look down the large breathing tubes and by which he can detect certain illnesses and take samples for testing (biopsy).

Brucellosis

An infectious disease caught by contact with infected cattle, goats or sheep or their milk. It is widespread throughout the world where milk is not sterilised. In the UK it occurs occasionally in veterinarians and workers on farms. In the Mediterranean it is known as Malta fever.

It is characterised by chronic fatigue, intermittent fever and aches and pains. As symptoms are vague, it is difficult to diagnose and should be considered whenever there is unexplained, persistent fever. People in rural areas or on holiday abroad should avoid drinking unpasteurised milk. Frequent veterinary inspection and testing of cattle are important for the prevention of this distressing disease.

Treatment is by specific antibiotics for 2–3 weeks.

Bruises

Caused by violence which does not break the skin, but injures the tissues. Colour changes are due to bleeding into the damaged tissues. The only treatment is time, which brings a return to normal. If painful a cold compress – lint wrung out in ice-cold water – helps. A black eye is one variety of bruise. The proverbial beef steak is no use. In children a loving cuddle is often the best medicine.

Bunion
(*See* BURSA.)

Burns
Injury caused by excessive heat to part of the body so as to damage or kill the tissues. It may be due to a flame, a hot object, excessive sunlight, or boiling water when the condition is called a SCALD. There is no practical difference between a burn and scald. Burns may also be caused by chemicals. In mild cases there may be only reddening of the skin (first degree). In second degree there is blistering, and in third degree, the whole skin thickness is destroyed, and the area appears charred. There are two chief dangers. First is *shock*, a severe form of collapse which follows extensive burns. Second is infection. When the tissues are killed or injured they cannot defend against invasion by germs, so that burns easily become infected and 'fester'. The *immediate* home treatment of burns (dry or wet) is to cool in cold running water; damage and pain can thus be reduced. Continue cooling until there is no further pain (up to thirty minutes if necessary). If the burn is severe or large (e.g. a blistered area more than 1″ (25mm) across in a child or 3″ (75mm) in an adult) shock should be treated by wrapping unburned areas with extra clothing or a blanket and giving a warm, sugared drink if patient is conscious. Urgent medical treatment is required for large burns but *initial cooling is always necessary*. Smaller burns can be covered by a freshly laundered handkerchief. Later they can be dressed with acriflex cream or betadine spray and covered with a non-stick Melolin dressing. Do not apply creams. If 'festering' occurs, consult your doctor who may give antibiotics.

Bursa *(Bursitis)*
A small sac containing fluid which protects part of the body from injury. It is usually found over some prominent bone which it cushions. If a bursa becomes

63

inflamed it is known as *bursitis*. This most commonly occurs in the feet, elbows and knees. There is a small bursa at the base of each of the big toes on the inner side. This commonly becomes inflamed through wearing too tight shoes and is often known as a BUNION. If protected from pressure by wearing loose shoes or slippers, it will often subside. A small pad round the bunion may help. Where symptoms ascribed to bunions are in fact due to rigidity of the toe joints (*hallux rigidus*), foot exercises such as picking up marbles or bean bags with the toes may help.

In a true bunion the bursa may become infected and discharge pus. The treatment is rest, heat and antibiotics. An operation may be the best way of preventing further trouble. Final results are usually good although a long convalescence with several weeks hobbling on crutches will have to be endured. Bunions are agony; worse than toothache and those who wear tight shoes will probably pay a painful price. Every child should be allowed enough room for the foot to grow within the shoe. Parents must keep a watchful eye to see that the toes do not become cramped.

In the knee there is a bursa over the knee-cap which may become inflamed if much kneeling is done (housemaid's knee). This subsides with rest, and it may be necessary to avoid kneeling. Exercising the parts, but not to the extent of agony, can help to dissipate adhesions and prevent recurrence. A knee or elbow arthro-pad worn for a day or two (not regularly because of weakening effect on muscles) may help. This should be obtainable at good chemists.

C

Caesarian Section (*See* BIRTH.)

Calculus
The medical term for 'stone'. Stones may form in organs
such as the gall bladder, kidneys or the urinary bladder,
and cause pain and other disturbances. Once a stone has
formed and causes trouble, removal by an operation is
generally necessary. Some small kidney stones can be
treated by external shock waves. Drugs are now available
which dissolve gall stones but recurrence after stopping
treatment may be a problem. (*See* GALL BLADDER, KIDNEY
DISEASES *and* RENAL COLIC.)

Cancer (*See also* LEUKAEMIA *and* CERVIX.)
This condition is all too common, and is the second most
frequent cause of death. The term 'cancer' covers a group
of allied disorders which have in common the un-
restrained growth of some small part of the body with the
formation of a lump or tumour. Normally the growth of
any particular part of the body is carefully regulated to
meet with its requirements. When some part is injured
the cells (minute living structures) of which it is composed multiply until the injury is made good, but the
whole process is controlled. In the condition of cancer,
for some reason, a group of cells starts to multiply abnormally and continues to do so, disorganising the normal
working of the body. Sometimes groups of these cells
may be carried to distant parts of the body by the blood
and there set up fresh tumours. If the process continues
unchecked some vital organ will eventually become so
disorganised that life cannot continue. It is vital *the lay
person should not take the all-too-common view that*

65

cancer is incurable. In many cases it is curable if taken early. The most effective treatment, in numerous instances, is still surgery, which means cutting out the affected part.

If all the cancer cells are removed the condition will be cured. The smaller the tumour, the less chance it has had to spread, and the more likely is complete cure.

There are also other valuable means of treatment such as radiotherapy, anti-tumour drugs, and certain hormones. Research indicates that some cancers are due to chemicals in the environment. Perhaps the greatest hope is prevention. Methods for detecting and identifying cancer-producing chemicals are being developed and will help to clean up our surroundings. Sources are industrial waste, car exhausts and cigarette smoke. New treatments being developed include high energy irradiation such as neutron beams. New drugs and new combinations of old drugs are showing promise in some cancers.

The illness is not common before 40 and the incidence increases with age. Perhaps the cells become less efficient at dealing with injury due to irritants over this age. **THE KEYNOTE OF SUCCESS IS EARLY DIAGNOSIS AND TREATMENT**. Anyone who has a symptom which does not go inside a few weeks should consult a doctor. Danger signals are a lump in breast (*see* BREAST) or testicle, etc., persistent cough (more than three weeks), persistent change in bowel habit, loss of weight, persistent or recurrent pain and the appearance of blood, for example from the bowels, in urine, from the mouth after coughing or vomiting, from the nipple or from the vagina after the menopause or between periods. The chances are there may be some other explanation which your doctor will be able to put right. If your doctor is suspicious he will be able to advise tests to establish the diagnosis.

Car Sickness (*See* TRAVEL SICKNESS.)

Carbuncle

Similar to a boil but the infection is deeper. A boil discharges through one opening; a carbuncle may have several. For a small carbuncle the treatment is similar (*see* BOILS) but for most consult a doctor.

Cardiac

Pertaining to the heart. (*See* HEART DISEASE.)

Cardiac Massage

This technique, more properly known as External Chest Compression, is used to create a circulation of oxygenated blood around the body of a patient whose heart has stopped beating. It must always be accompanied by ARTIFICIAL RESPIRATION (*see pages 39–43*). The function of cardiac massage is not to restart the heart but to buy time by acting as a 'life support machine' until an ambulance arrives.

Cartilage

A pad of 'gristle' in many joints which acts as a buffer between bones. The common one to cause trouble is in the knee. A twist may cause it to tear with acute pain in the knee which often becomes locked and swollen. The symptoms may subside with rest, but often the cartilage needs to be removed by a simple operation to save further trouble. It may be worth wearing a knee support pad for a few days while trying the resting cure.

Cataract

A condition, usually occurring in older people, in which the lens of the eye becomes clouded (*see page 112*), so that less light reaches the retina. Vision becomes progressively worse but the outlook is good if removed. Sometimes the condition becomes arrested, or affects one eye only. In any case it is possible to operate and remove the opacity. Usually an artificial lens is inserted at the time of operation. Otherwise thick glasses must be worn after the operation to focus the light.

Catarrh

A rather vague term but usually taken to mean a stuffed-up feeling in head and nose, with or without nasal discharge and is sometimes associated with a feeling of sticky fluid dripping down the back of the throat. These symptoms are normal in the week or two following a cold or flu. Children tend to have twice as many colds as adults and thus in winter may seem to have persistent snuffles and catarrh. A constant running nose and mouth-breathing in a child may indicate large adenoids. Many 'catarrhal' children however out-grow the condition at about seven years as their nasal passages enlarge and become less easily blocked. A foul nasal discharge in a child suggests a foreign body e.g. a bead, stuck in the nose.

The catarrh which follows a cold can be relieved by inhaling the vapour of Friars' Balsam (one teaspoonful to a pint of boiling water). If catarrh persists for more than three weeks after a cold there may be underlying sinusitis which can be treated by your doctor. *(See* ANTRUM.)

Allergy such as hay fever causes watery catarrh, frequent sneezing and 'stuffed-up' nose. Allergic subjects tend to develop nasal polyps (thickened folds of the lining of the nose) which increase the catarrh. The piece of cartilage which divides the nasal passages is deviated to one side in some people. Stuffiness and blockage can then occur on the narrow side. This can be helped by a minor operation.

Other causes of catarrh include *smoking,* a polluted or damp atmosphere and *excessive use of nose drops.*

Catheter

A tube for withdrawing fluid from a cavity – e.g. the bladder.

Cellulitis

A spreading skin infection due to a germ. The area affected becomes red, swollen and painful, and the patient usually has fever. Get expert treatment, for it is usually rapidly curable with antibiotics.

Cerebral
Pertaining to the brain. (*See* STROKE.)

Cervical Spondylosis
Osteoarthritis occurring in the neck joints. Symptoms may include aching and stiffness in the neck as well as pain, weakness and 'pins and needles' in the arms when the nerves emerging through canals in the vertebrae in the neck become irritated by pressure from swollen joints. A collar of foam or plastic, worn for one to three months, will usually bring relief, as may exercise, traction, manipulation and radiant heat. (*See* ARTHRITIS *and* OSTEOARTHRITIS.)

Cervix (*See* BIRTH, CONTRACEPTION *and* INFERTILITY.)
The neck of the womb which opens in childbirth. Cancer of the cervix is a common but, hopefully, preventable form of cancer in women and can occur at a relatively young age. An easy test (cervical smear) is useful in detecting early changes. The procedure takes seconds and is no more uncomfortable than an internal examination. The smear is examined in a laboratory and altered cells can be spotted before they have invaded other tissues (i.e. become malignant).

Early disease can be treated by removing part of the cervix (coning). In other cases hysterectomy (removal of the womb) is performed and the patient is carefully followed up.

Extreme care in hygiene of the penis and underside of the foreskin is vital as it is thought the 'debris' which collects may contribute to cervical cancer.

Chancre (*See* SYPHILIS.)

Change of Life (*See* MENOPAUSE.)

Chicken Pox (*See also* SHINGLES.)

One of the infective illnesses of childhood, caused by a virus. Most children catch it, usually during school years. A second attack is rare. Incubation is usually about two to three weeks, i.e. it takes that time for symptoms to develop after invasion by the virus. Sometimes the child is off colour before the spots develop, but usually spots are the first symptoms. At first they are small red bumps, but develop a white top containing fluid and later form a crust. The spots usually appear on the chest, and spread to the face, scalp, the upper parts of limbs and may appear in the mouth. The child may have a slight fever, and is infectious for seven days after the spots appear. Complications of chicken pox are rare (though it can be worse in adults) and uneventful recovery the rule. The same germ can cause shingles later in life.

Chilblain

A red, painful itching area on the extremities after exposure to cold. (Most often on feet, hands and nose.) It is usually associated with poor circulation. Those subject to chilblains should take care in cold weather, wearing warm socks and gloves. Extremities should not be warmed suddenly, at the fire or in hot water, after being cold, as this may worsen the condition. Vasodilator tablets (which open up the small blood vessels) such as 'Pernivit' are helpful if taken regularly after meals in winter.

Choking

Choking occurs when a blockage (usually food) becomes lodged in the back of the airway. If the blockage is small, the patient will cough and expel the blockage for himself (sometimes with the help of a slap on the back). If the blockage is larger, it may completely block the airway and the patient will not be able to speak, breathe or cough – he will typically clutch his throat and start to become blue from lack of oxygen.

To remove the obstruction first try leaning the patient forwards and give up to five firm blows on the back, between the shoulder blades. If these do not work, you should perform abdominal thrusts. Place your arms around the patient from behind. Make one hand into a fist and place this just under the rib cage. Place the other hand on top and pull upwards and inwards towards you. Repeat this up to five times. Alternate five back blows with five abdominal thrusts until the blockage is ejected from the mouth.

If you are alone and choking, you can try to perform abdominal thrusts on yourself or bend suddenly over the back of a chair to try to force yourself to breathe out.

To reduce the risk of choking, small children should not be given nuts, boiled sweets or small toys. For a child who is choking, hold him face down across your knees (or along your arm if it is a baby) and give five firm blows between the shoulder blades, ensuring that the head is lower than the chest while you do this. If this does not work, try up to five chest thrusts, using a similar technique to chest compressions (see page 42) but at a slower rate. If these fail, abdominal thrusts (using less force than for an adult) can be used for children over one year. For children less than one year, only use chest thrusts with just two fingers to exert pressure.

Cholera

An infectious disease marked by severe watery diarrhoea which leads to fluid depletion, cramps and collapse. It needs urgent medical care. It is caused by a germ invading the bowels and can be spread by contaminated water supplies. It occurs in epidemics particularly in Asia, Africa and the Mediterranean so it is important for travellers to these and any other risky areas to be inoculated. However, vaccinations provide partial protection; the best prevention is scrupulous care over food and drink (especially drinking water, shellfish and uncooked food).

Cholesterol

A fatty substance which circulates in the blood. High levels result in premature deposits on the lining of the arteries and heart disease. Because cholesterol is a constituent of animal fat most people would be wise to reduce the intake of animal fat. Vegetable oils and fatty fish are low in cholesterol. (*See* ARTERIOSCLEROSIS *and* HEART DISEASE.)

Chorea

Popularly known as St Vitus' Dance. It is now rare in the UK. It may occur in children and adolescents following a throat infection. (*See* RHEUMATIC FEVER.) Uncontrolled movements occur due to a temporary brain disturbance. Treatment is bed rest during the acute stage and a prolonged course of antibiotics. The outcome is usually good.

Circumcision

Surgical removal of the male foreskin – practised as a Jewish or other religious rite. In the UK it is generally considered unnecessary as most infants have a fully retractable foreskin by six. The foreskin helps to protect the glans-penis from napkin irritation. After this, daily washing beneath the foreskin should prevent inflammation or infection. If the foreskin opening appears to be pinhole size, or ballooning occurs when water is passed or there are repeated attacks of balanitis – circumcision may be necessary on medical grounds. Do not attempt to pull back the foreskin before three or four years. It is not yet free and over-enthusiastic attempts to do this could cause scars or pain. In desert countries the risk of sand under the foreskin may justify circumcision. (*See* BALANITIS.)

Cirrhosis

Disease of the liver marked by deterioration of the cells and formation of hard scar tissue. There are many causes. (*See* ALCOHOLISM.)

Cleft Palate

During development of a baby in the womb the roof of the mouth is split, and the upper lip has two splits which normally join before birth. If the roof of the mouth fails to join, the condition is known as cleft palate; the lip as harelip. These may interfere with feeding; a prompt operation should rectify. In severe cases further surgery is required and there should be little problem with speech as long as speech therapy is provided early.

Cold (*Coryza*)

A frequent illness in civilised communities due to virus infection; not dangerous in itself but occasionally the forerunner of serious bronchitis, pneumonia, etc. (See below.) If you have a cold, avoid mixing as viruses spread in crowded, muggy conditions. Low temperature does not seem to cause colds and probably their prevalence is due to living together in *poorly ventilated, over-heated conditions*. The best treatment is a day or two in bed. Two soluble aspirins or Paracetamol may be taken up to four times a day. Keep the patient warm, diet light, fluids plentiful. Gargles and lemon or honey drinks soothe, whisky is a pleasant night-cap but little more. The virus does not respond to antibiotics so do not request these unless you suffer asthma, bronchitis or heart disease. Complications include sinusitis and bronchitis. (*See* ANTRUM, BRONCHITIS *and* CATARRH.) Vitamin C has been tried as a cold preventive. Whilst it may increase resistance there is no real evidence it is effective.

There is no scientific proof, but avoiding draughts, changing into dry clothing if soaked and avoiding too many late nights *appear* to reduce the incidence of colds, perhaps because resistance is stronger. A cold lasts two weeks if treated and fourteen days if not!

Colic
Griping intermittent abdominal pain which may occur with food, poisoning, appendicitis, etc. Originally referred only to pain in the colon (large bowel) but now used to describe sharp periodic pain in many organs. Adults should see a doctor for investigation if it is persistent or recurrent. Colic as indicated by screaming attacks is common in infants and babies and is often due to feeding problems.

Colitis
Inflammation of the colon (the large terminal portion of the bowel – *see Fig. 1, page 35*). Usually associated with abdominal pain, and diarrhoea, accompanied by mucus (slime) or even blood. Ulcerative colitis is one serious and debilitating form. Many drugs are available to help. Occasionally part of the bowel may have to be removed if colitis persists and an ileostomy is performed. (*See* ILEOSTOMY.)

Colostomy
The surgical manufacture of a new opening of the large bowel on the surface of the abdomen. This is necessary after removal of a large part of diseased bowel. The motions are discharged into disposable polythene bags. Improved surgical methods have resulted in regular and predictable bowel action in many cases, so the sufferer rarely needs to tolerate a soiled bag for long. Earlier problems of erratic motions and odour have largely been overcome. The Colostomy Welfare Group exists to help sufferers with this condition. (*See* ILEOSTOMY.)

Coma
A state of unconsciousness, lasting more than a few minutes, from which the patient cannot be roused even by powerful stimulation. There are many causes such as overdose of drugs or alcohol, diseases or injuries to the brain. The layman should send at once for medical aid.

The patient should be made comfortable and kept warm. *Give nothing* since trying to force liquids down the throat of an unconscious person will usually result in choking. Anything tight should be removed from the neck, and the patient observed to see if he is breathing. If not, artificial respiration may be necessary. (*See* ASPHYXIA *and* ARTIFICIAL RESPIRATION.)

Concussion
Brain injury produced by jarring violence to the head which may result in dazing, vomiting or unconsciousness (*see* COMA). Severe concussion may be associated with other injuries such as fractured skull, and is often followed by some loss of memory (*see* AMNESIA) and headaches. Urgently call a doctor and ambulance for a severe head injury. If the patient is unconscious treat, until help arrives, as for coma.

Symptoms to take seriously even if the head injury *seems* trivial include being 'knocked out' even for a second or so, nausea and vomiting, double vision, pallor and clamminess. In these circumstances the patient should be taken to a hospital casualty department.

Congenital Dislocation of the Hip
A few babies are born with dislocated hip joints. Fortunately this is now routinely tested for in the West, and, once detected, is usually cured after the wearing of a splint for a few months. (*See* LIMP.)

Conjunctivitis
Inflammation of the delicate membrane lining the eye and the inside of the lids. It results in redness especially at the corners of the eye and watery or sticky discharge. The lids may be stuck together in the mornings. The condition is often due to infection but may also be caused by chemicals or allergy (hay fever). Mild symptoms may respond to bathing with salt solution (1

teaspoon of salt to 1 pint of water), but a *painful* eye needs urgent medical advice as other serious conditions may be present. Any eye problem should always be shown to a doctor. Treatment of the usual infective conjunctivitis is by antibiotic eyedrops. (*See also* EYES.)

Constipation

This occurs when the bowel motions are hard and passed infrequently or with difficulty. Healthy bowel action is easy and regular although there is a great variation in the frequency of movements – from perhaps twice to thrice daily down to one every three days. What matters is the ease with which the motion is passed.

Lack of fibre and exercise, also the rush to work sometimes ignoring the call to evacuate, are the usual causes of constipation. It may be made worse by the regular use of laxatives as the bowels become less sensitive.

Constipation can generally be corrected by a couple of teaspoons of powdered bran sprinkled on a cereal daily, fruit, vegetables, more exercise and time in the morning to accommodate the bowel habit. Occasional laxatives may be necessary if travelling to where the water or food supply differs. Regular laxatives may be essential for a few but only on medical advice. *Report any persistent change in bowel habits.*

Children after potty training should be encouraged and given time to open the bowels daily after breakfast. Encourage children to eat a diet rich in fruit, fibre and vegetables. *Aperients should not be given to children unless on a doctor's instructions.*

Contraception
The Pill

Contraception was revolutionised in the 'fifties by the development and use of synthetic female hormones (*see* HORMONES) which act as contraceptives; their main action is to prevent release of the egg to the Fallopian tube.

Family planning is covered by our National Health Service and advice can be obtained from local clinics or most family doctors. Similar arrangements exist abroad.

A medical check is needed before the pill can be prescribed. A history of thrombosis, high blood pressure or recent jaundice rules it out. During diarrhoea or vomiting, the pill may pass too quickly to be effective so extra precautions such as the sheath should be used then. Varicose veins or migraine can be made worse. Generally women over 35 who smoke should consider choosing another method but *be guided by your doctor*. After starting the pill you need to be seen three-monthly at first for check-up and thereafter once a year.

Most pills are taken once daily for *three* weeks out of four. Take the pill at the same time (usually bedtime) as varying the time can lead to spotting of blood from the vagina. In the *fourth* week there is a small painless 'period' when the womb sheds its lining. This prevents 'build-up' and provides reassurance that pregnancy has not occurred. Most side effects are minor and explained in leaflets in the packs. *If in doubt about a symptom, you must see your doctor*. Extra vitamin B6 can often reverse any lack of sex drive or depression. Check with your doctor if any additional medicines are prescribed. Treatments such as antibiotics can reduce the effectiveness of the pill. This may be indicated by spotting of blood from the vagina which should not generally happen after the first two months. Take additional precautions (e.g. the sheath) when this happens.

There is a slightly increased risk of blood clotting from the oestrogen component of the pill although risk is less than that in a pregnancy. The increased risk applies mainly to women over 35 who smoke.

A pill containing progestogen only is suitable for

many women, especially those who are breast feeding and the over 40s. The effectiveness is only slightly less; periods may be erratic. This low dose pill lets women continue the pill until the menopause.

'Morning after' – 'Emergency' only

If unprotected intercourse (e.g. a sheath bursts) occurs, a 'morning after' pill can be taken. This usually prevents the fertilised egg from embedding in the womb. Embedding, not fertilisation, is the hallmark of pregnancy, so this method may be counted contraceptive and not abortive. To have maximum effect this pill must be taken within twelve hours of intercourse (but it may be effective for up to 36 hours after intercourse) and a family planning clinic or doctor *must be urgently* consulted. The dose of hormone in the 'morning after' pill is high so this method must be reserved for rare 'emergency' use. An IUD (see next paragraph) inserted within four or five days of intercourse acts similarly.

Copper or Plastic Device (IUD)

Many women do not like taking tablets on a long-term basis and insertion of a copper or plastic device into the womb may be their ideal solution. Insertion is seldom painful when done by a trained doctor. The intra uterine device (IUD) once in place needs attention from the patient who should be instructed how to feel the threads in the vagina at intervals. Regular checks (annually unless otherwise instructed) should also take place by a trained doctor or nurse.

The IUD is not quite as reliable as the pill and may cause heavier periods. A few women are unable to retain them and tend to expel them with cramping pains shortly after insertion.

With the new advances in hormones it tends to be forgotten that the simple barrier methods are still very effective if used properly.

The Sheath

The sheath (condom) has a success rate comparable to the IUD if combined with a sperm-killing chemical. It is more convenient for the woman to take responsibility for the chemical. The sheath is also valuable in that it affords some protection against venereal disease whereas the pill has probably contributed to its spreading.

The Cap Method

There is a similar success rate for the female barrier methods of diaphragm or cervical cap also combined with chemicals. These caps must be fitted by a doctor and checked at regular intervals. Some kinds are shown in Fig. 4.

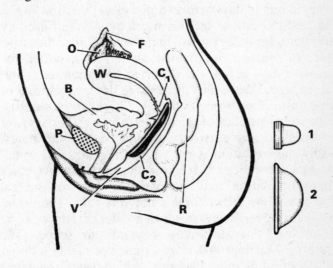

Fig. 4 Contraception Cap

F	Fallopian Tube	B	Bladder
O	Ovary	P	Pubic Bone
W	Womb	R	Rectum
C_1	Cervix – opening to womb	1	Cervical Cap
C_2	Cap (Diaphragm or Dutch Cap)	2	Diaphragm or Dutch Cap
V	Vagina		

Chemical methods alone are not reliable although Delfen Foam is more effective than most.

The Safe Period (Rhythm Method)

The method accepted by Roman Catholics. Unfortunately it has not lived up to early hopes. Being natural it is the perfect birth control but *for its unreliability*. Nevertheless for couples who want, say a 2½ year gap between children but who would not worry were the gap only 12 to 20 months, or for newly married people hoping to wait a few years before parenthood, but whom an earlier conception would not distress, it is excellent. Also, *as an additional method to another*, e.g. the sheath, it has value. The method is based on the fact that the ovum is expected to be released by the ovary about 14 days *before* (note *before*) the first day of the next period. As the ovum can only be fertilised by the sperm for a day or two, in *theory*, all other dates are safe. In practice, intercourse should be avoided, for say, five days before the expected ovulation date, and the expected date, plus three more days, i.e. a total of nine days, (five + one + three). Checks to be sure the woman has periods of regular length (e.g. 28 days) are essential to arrive at what should be the safe dates. Sadly the ovulation is not always regular, and sometimes a second egg is released the next day. At other times, ovulation may be early or late for several reasons. Thus the method is not very safe. There are, however, several ways in which greater certainty can be employed, but all this is beyond our scope. The Catholic Marriage Advisory Council produces a booklet 'Natural Family Planning' which gives the latest information. The BMA sells a booklet 'Contraception Choice Not Chance'.

The Family Planning Association, or the equivalent in most lands, is able to help with birth control problems as should your doctor.

The Sponge Method

A soft circular sponge impregnated with spermicide can be bought from the chemist or is available from some family planning clinics. Instruction in its proper use is recommended.

Withdrawal

Coitus interruptus (where the man withdraws from the vagina just before ejaculation), although not completely satisfactory either for sexual harmony or as a method of contraception, is widely practised. It is not a safe method partly because the man often withdraws too late; it is almost impossible not to sometimes, despite what some men imagine. More important – sperms can be present in the urethra before ejaculation.

Sterilisation *(See Fig. 5 overleaf.)*
Male Sterilisation *(Vasectomy)*

The vas deferens (sperm tube) is divided and the ends tied. It takes several weeks (even months) after the operation for sperm to disappear totally from the ejaculate.

Female Sterilisation

The Fallopian tubes, down which the ovum (egg) travels from the ovary to be fertilised, are divided and the ends tied.

Many couples are turning to sterilisation when they think their family is complete. This allows the woman to leave off the pill before the age at which most of the complications occur. It also avoids the problems of heavy periods caused by the IUD in the forties at a stage when the monthly losses tend to be greater. The couple must think the implications through and usually have no regrets. Never forget that circumstances could arise in which you may want to have children again.

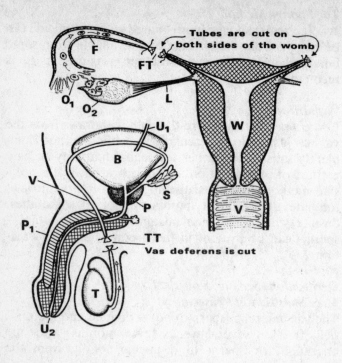

Fig. 5 Sterilisation

	Male		Female
V	'Sperm tube' called vas deferens	**F**	Fallopian tube
TT	Vas deferens is tied and cut	**FT**	Fallopian tube tied and cut
U₁	Ureter from kidneys (carries urine from kidney to bladder)	**L**	Ligament of ovary (keeps ovary in place)
B	Bladder		
P₁	Penis	**O₁**	Ovum released from ovary
U₂	Opening of urethra (tube from bladder to penis)	**O₂**	Ovary
P	Prostate gland	**W**	Womb
S	Seminal vesicles (secrete fluid to keep sperm alive and moving)	**V**	Vagina

Convulsion

Loss of consciousness with twitching or jerking movement of part or all the body; often known as a 'fit'. Fits sometimes occur in young children with high temperature, and under these conditions are not necessarily serious. Children who have had one feverish convulsion should be given Paracetamol and tepid sponging during any subsequent feverish illness such as tonsillitis or a heavy cold. The danger time is after four p.m. (1600 hours) when temperatures start to rise for the night. If a fit does occur, lie the child on his side in a place where he cannot harm himself on furniture, etc. Most feverish fits last only a few minutes but the doctor should be called urgently in case the twitching persists and the child requires a sedative injection. Feverish fits generally cease by the age of five. (*See* EPILEPSY.)

Corns
Small areas of painful, compressed thickened skin usually on the toes and largely due to ill-fitting shoes. Corn pads and salt water soaks ease the pain but the best treatment may be skilled chiropody by a Chiropodist (State Registered in the UK).

Coronary Thrombosis
This is more commonly known as 'heart attack' and occurs when a blood vessel (coronary artery) supplying the heart becomes blocked by a clot (*see* ANGINA PECTORIS).

The patient suffering a heart attack will look pale, grey and sweaty. He will have a persistent, crushing pain in his chest, often feeling like a tight band or heavy weight on the chest. The pain will not subside and will often radiate to the neck, jaw and arms (especially the left arm) with numbness or tingling of the fingers. The patient will often be short of breath and may feel nauseous or be sick. It is also typical that the patient will try to deny that there is a serious problem, saying that the pain is 'just indigestion'.

A heart attack is a serious medical emergency – those

who die of heart attacks usually do so within the first two hours of the onset of symptoms. If you suspect a heart attack, you must call for an ambulance immediately, describing the symptoms and saying you suspect a heart attack.

Whilst you wait for the ambulance to arrive, sit the patient down leaning against the wall with his knees bent. Loosen tight clothing and keep reassuring him. Do not allow him to move and do not give him anything to eat or drink. If the patient becomes unconscious before the ambulance arrives you may need to commence resuscitation (*see* ARTIFICIAL RESPIRATION).

The blocked artery stops blood containing oxygen and nourishment reaching part of the heart muscle. This area of muscle is damaged and is eventually replaced by a firm scar. During recovery the aim is to ensure that the remaining healthy heart muscle can cope.

Patients found to have high blood pressure or cholesterol levels are put on a low animal fat diet and given appropriate tablets. They should stop smoking (*see* SMOKING, *page 16*) and aim to lose any excess weight. Alcohol, a mild heart poison, should be avoided.

Convalescent patients should aim at gradually increasing exercise such as walking, or special exercises provided in a heart clinic gymnasium, until restored to normal activities.

Previously inactive subjects should walk when possible and keep car driving to a minimum. Most can resume sexual intercourse some eight to twelve weeks after an uncomplicated coronary.

There is no sure way to prevent a coronary thrombosis. Plenty of exercise, a low fat and low sugar diet, no smoking, little or no alcohol, a free and easy attitude, all help, but some families have a worse record than others. If you have a bad family record for heart disease it is worth asking your doctor to check your blood pressure and blood cholesterol. If these are normal, forget the subject and enjoy life, but avoid smoking.

Cot Death *(Sudden Infant Death Syndrome)*
The term for sudden death in babies under a year, usually around three to five months. No single cause has been found although often the child has apparently had a trivial 'cold' for a few days. Acute allergy has been suggested, but it does seem that in some cases an apparently insignificant infection has suddenly proved fatal. Much support is needed for parents who suffer needless guilt feelings.

Breast-fed babies are less likely to get infections and allergy than are the bottle-fed so this seems another good reason to promote breast feeding. Solid foods which can cause allergy are best avoided until the baby is four months old. It has recently been shown that a substantial reduction in the death rate has followed the instruction to lie babies on their backs in their cots or prams.

Coughing Blood
(*See* HAEMOPTYSIS.)

Cramp
A condition due to a painful muscle spasm, often associated with exposure to cold. It may attack swimmers who have been in the water too long. Treat by 'straightening' the cramped part and vigorously rubbing the sore muscle to warm it and restore circulation. In hot climates cramp may be due to lack of salt. Taking more salt with the diet may be essential; salt tablets are available for this purpose. Cramp endangers swimmers but is less likely to occur if bathing is postponed 1½ hours after meals. (It is safer to stay within one's depth.) Leg cramps at night are usually associated with poor circulation and respond well to quinine bisulphate tablets which, because of

side effects, should be taken only under doctor's orders.

Cretin

A rare condition in which babies born with a defective thyroid gland develop mental and physical deficiency. Early treatment can prevent mental retardation and other problems.

Croup

An infective condition resulting from partial obstruction of the larynx (voice box) occurring chiefly in children and characterised by barking cough, hoarseness and breathing difficulty. Infection causes swelling of the larynx lining so that the small air passage becomes blocked. Relief can be obtained in a steamy atmosphere provided by a kettle in the room. Call a doctor if there is any degree of breathing distress. The child tends to grow out of this as the voice box becomes larger and less easily blocked. Experienced mothers can cope with milder attacks on their own by the use of steam. However, breathing distress occurring for the first time in a young child needs urgent medical attention.

Cyst

A collection of fluid in a part of the body. A common cyst in the skin is due to fluid in a blocked oil-producing gland. This is known as a sebaceous cyst or wen and the best treatment is surgical removal – a tiny operation. If left cysts may become infected and cause trouble.

Cystitis

Medical term for bladder inflammation, usually accompanied by severe pain and frequency in passing water.

The bladder lies low in the abdomen and receives the urine from the kidneys. Sometimes germs enter the bladder and cause infection and inflammation.

Cystitis is much more common in women because the germs which often cause it come from the bowel; the openings from the bladder and the bowels are closer in the female. To avoid cystitis women should take particular care in their personal hygiene. Some patients find it helps (and saves fuel) to take showers rather than baths (bowel germs are present in static bath water). After emptying the bowels, toilet paper should be employed in a front to back direction; not the reverse. Stockings and cotton pants are preferable to tights. Symptoms often follow sexual intercourse and sufferers should always empty the bladder immediately after intercourse. Patients with symptoms should take a urine sample (the portion caught in midstream) in a sterile container (boiled bottle will do) to their doctor to test. Tests may confirm the usual bowel germ (E. Coli) is present. A short course of antibiotics usually cures. In the meantime, plenty of fluids (five to six pints of water daily) and an alkali such as potassium citrate mixture, one tablespoon in half a tumbler of water three times a day, will soothe.

Recurrent attacks or failure to clear might indicate need for further investigation.

Some patients with recurrent symptoms never show evidence of germs. The problem may be one of chemicals or rubber sensitivity due to contraceptives, perfumed bath products or deodorants.

Some women fear venereal disease as symptoms often occur in the early months of intercourse. Although this is usually not the cause they should voice these worries to their doctor or attend a special clinic so that a few extra simple tests can be performed.

After the menopause the tissues around the bladder exit and front passage become delicate and easily inflamed so that cystitis may again become common.

Oestrogen creams often help the other treatments here.

Even a single attack of cystitis in a child needs specialist investigation to ensure that infection is not passing upwards into the kidney tubes leading from the bladder.

D

Deafness

There are two types. One is due to inadequacy of the nerve endings in the ear (cochlea) and the other is due to impaired conduction of sound through the 'sound-box' of the ear. Nerve deafness may be present at birth or result from head injury, exposure to excessive noise (in industry, airports, noisy warehouse, music, shooting, the 'pop' world, etc.) and virus infections. It is also the deafness which occurs gradually with advancing years, although it can affect some individuals earlier in life than average. *Noise-produced deafness should be preventable.* It is regrettable that many workers in noisy occupations fail to wear the protective ear pads provided. Otherwise the only treatment is to amplify residual hearing by a hearing aid. The National Health Service now provides neat behind-the-ear aids.

In the UK babies are tested for hearing at seven months and thereafter at pre-school and infant school checks. If you have any doubts about your child's hearing, tell your doctor at once so that further tests can be carried out. Normal hearing is necessary for the development of speech.

Conduction deafness can be due to various conditions of the middle and outer ear. Germs may enter the ear (connected by a tube with the throat), following a cold or other infection. These will cause inflammation and temporary deafness. Nowadays antibiotics will cure the infections but occasionally catarrhal or glue-like fluid and deafness persists. Such a patient – usually a child – needs to be checked after treatment for middle ear infection in case this fluid needs draining by a specialist. Sometimes special tubes known as grommets are used. There must be no swimming whilst the tubes are in place. Intermittent or doubtful deafness should be taken seriously in a child as the condition is likely to be due to fluid or 'glue' which may not settle spontaneously.

Although the eardrum may perforate in an infection it usually heals quickly with modern treatment. Occasionally a perforation may not heal and the ear may discharge at intervals for years. The combination of imperfect drum and discharge in the middle ear causes deafness. Some perforations can now be repaired surgically.

Otosclerosis
If the small bones in the ear harden (otosclerosis) there is again a form of conduction deafness. This condition worsens in pregnancy and sometimes on the 'pill' and these points should be carefully considered by any sufferer. Surgery may help but not always. In several forms of conduction deafness, where surgery can do no more, the hearing aid has a large part to play.

In severe deafness, lip reading may be the best means for communication. Classes are unfortunately few, but details can be had from the Royal National Institute for the Deaf.

Syringing the ear is only of value if wax is present in the outer canal. This is common and fortunately easy to cure. (*See* EARACHE, OTITIS MEDIA, TINNITUS *and* WAX.)

Death
The layman is sometimes confronted with death. One urgent question is, has death occurred, or is there a possibility of help? Urgently check if breathing (even slight) continues, check for heart beats and note if the body is stiff or cold. To test breathing, look carefully at the chest to see if it moves; if in doubt, hold a mirror,

failing which a piece of glass, close to the mouth and nostrils to see if it becomes clouded. If beating, the heart may be heard by placing one ear on the chest in the region of the left nipple, or the pulse may be felt for on the front of the wrist just below the base of the thumb. If there is no breathing, no heart beat, and particularly if the body is stiff or cold, death has occurred. If there is a sign of life treat the patient as for shock (*see* SHOCK) until medical aid arrives. If necessary the kiss of life must be tried while awaiting help. (*See* ARTIFICIAL RESPIRATION *and* COT DEATH.)

Delirium
A state of restlessness, the patient being only partly conscious. Delirium usually accompanies a high fever, and the patient may throw himself about, pick at the bedclothes and mutter without ceasing. It may help, if the patient is conscious to give soluble aspirin or Paracetamol, and sponge him down with tepid water until the doctor arrives. This will reduce the temperature of the body, and often quieten the patient for a while. A special form of delirium known as *delirium tremens* is associated with alcoholism. (*See* ALCOHOLISM.)

Dementia *(Senile Dementia)*
Progressive condition of loss of intelligence often found in old age, sometimes caused by Alzheimer's disease. Hospital care may eventually be needed. (*See* MENTAL ILLNESS *and* OLD AGE.)

Dentures
Those who suffer from badly fitting artificial teeth should not put up with them. Return to your dentist and get a good set. If he cannot fit you, then change your dentist or get a set made privately.

If you have a good set, there should be no need to remove them at night, which is a morale-booster. Wash them night and morning and brush the gums. Some doctors would disagree but millions are not any the worse for retaining them. Small or part plates should be removed while asleep, due to danger of swallowing.

Painful biting may improve as the gums harden. For some foods you may need to use suction (consciously) and your tongue to prevent the teeth tipping forward. Progress to harder foods and ultimately you can aim to eat apples without quartering them.

Depression (*See* MENTAL ILLNESS.)
A condition which may include depressed mood, apathy, feelings of guilt, lack of physical energy and disturbed sleep. It always needs urgent attention especially in the early weeks after childbirth.

Dermatitis
Means inflammation of the skin and thus covers practically the whole range of skin diseases, but is usually used as an alternative to eczema. The lay idea that it is a 'dirty' condition is false. Common examples are contact dermatitis due to sensitivity to detergents or metals such as nickel. Barrier creams and gloves help to protect the skin. Hydrocortisone cream and other steroid creams reduce the inflammation and itchiness. Sufferers should avoid excess washing with soap or detergents.

Dextrose
A form of the quick-acting sugar glucose, useful to restore energy and prevent sleepiness in long distance drivers. (It is carried by diabetics to ward off sudden falls in blood sugar and prevent coma.)

Dhobie Itch
An itchy rash in the groins – more common in men. It is due to a fungal infection of the skin. (*See* ATHLETE'S FOOT *and* TINEA.)

Diabetes

In diabetes the body is unable to make proper use of carbohydrates or sugary foods. Normally carbohydrates undergo changes in the body with release of energy which the body can use. These changes are controlled by insulin, made by one of the internal glands, the pancreas. (*See Fig. 1, page 35.*) In diabetes the pancreas fails to make sufficient insulin so that sugar, instead of being properly used, accumulates. The kidneys try to get rid of this excess sugar so the patient passes more urine than normal, and often has a persistent thirst in consequence. Other symptoms include general ill health, a loss of weight and energy, itching of the skin and a liability to infections such as boils. There are two types of diabetes – one occurring in the young (insulin-dependent diabetes) and the other in older obese patients (non insulin-dependent diabetes).

The young diabetic always needs regular replacement insulin whereas the older patient may respond to diet restriction only or to diet plus tablets. These allow the patient to make the most of his limited supplies of natural insulin. Insulin must be given by injection since it is destroyed by digestive juices. Most diabetics (including many doctors!) can lead normal lives with one or two injections daily. They must have regular mealtimes and become familiar with their exercise tolerance, otherwise they tend to plunge into low blood sugar states. Once they and their doctors have got their diet, insulin requirement and exercise balanced, they can live full lives. Feelings of faintness, irritability or lack of concentration can indicate low blood sugar and diabetics always carry glucose tablets to combat this.

Diabetics usually carry a card or wear a medical bracelet stating their condition. If a person is found in a semi-conscious or 'drunk' state it is worth checking this. If he is sufficiently conscious to swallow sugar this may bring him round, otherwise urgent medical attention is needed.

Diarrhoea

A condition in which the stools are abnormally fluid, but is commonly used to describe when the bowels are opened more often than the normal. These conditions often occur together. There are many causes of diarrhoea. In children it may follow over-eating of fruit, but is usually due to infection. For mild diarrhoea it is best to live on liquids only for twenty-four hours e.g. dilute fruit juices or glucose solution – one dessertspoon to a pint of water plus a pinch of salt. Follow this by a light diet for the next day or two – no meat, vegetables or whole fruit for three days. If diarrhoea persists, if accompanied by a pain or a raised temperature, see a doctor. Babies (under one year) should be seen early by a doctor as they are susceptible to fluid loss and can become dangerously low in body fluid.

Diphtheria

A disease, once of world-wide distribution, now largely disappeared from Europe and North America due to vaccination.

It starts as a throat infection similar to tonsillitis and produces a membrane which may obstruct breathing. It also produces a poison which can damage the heart and nerves.

Any throat infection accompanied by high fever needs medical attention. It is unlikely to be diphtheria in the West unless the patient has recently been to Asia or Russia. If there is any reason for suspicion, throat swabs are taken and the patient isolated.

Diplopia

(*See* DOUBLE VISION.)

Discharge

Outpouring of fluid from a body opening e.g. from the nose during a cold. One cause of worry is discharge from the sex organs which may be due to venereal infection (*see* GONORRHOEA). There are other causes, especially in women, but any discharge of this nature should receive medical attention. There may be a harmless explanation, but neglect could be serious.

Dislocation
Occurs when a bone slips out of joint. It normally results from violence and may occur at almost any joint. Perhaps the most common is dislocation of the shoulder, when the rounded head of the humerus (the bone in the upper arm) slips out of its hollow in the shoulder. There is acute pain, and deformity. The unskilled should do nothing except make the patient comfortable and get medical help. Attempts to move the dislocated bone may damage the joint and must be avoided. The part affected may be supported, e.g. by a sling or cushion, until seen by a suitably qualified doctor.

Disseminated Sclerosis
(*See* MULTIPLE SCLEROSIS.)

Diverticulitis
Inflammation of the intestine due to small pockets which become irritated and infected forming in the walls of the bowel. Before inflammation and infection occur the condition may be controlled by a diet rich in fibre.

If infection occurs it can often be cured by antibiotics. Operation is rarely necessary.

Dog Bite *(including* **Rabies***)*
To be bitten by a dog can be dangerous because of transfer of infection. The most serious is the disease known as rabies (hydrophobia) which causes madness in dogs. Those bitten often acquire the infection and die painfully.

Rabies is transmitted by dogs and foxes. It is found all over the world but not in Australasia or the UK (thanks to strict quarantine rules). Human beings catch it by being bitten as it is found in the saliva. The disease causes acute muscle spasms, a form of madness and death unless treated early.

If abroad where rabies is endemic, avoid contact with animals, e.g. dogs, foxes, cats and hedgehogs. If scratched or bitten, First Aid treatment is of the utmost importance and consists of thoroughly cleaning the bitten area with detergent or concentrated soap. If a limb has been bitten, a tourniquet should be applied to encourage bleeding. A caustic substance should be applied to the area – such as permanganate of potash, acid or caustic soda. After this local treatment, urgent medical attention from a rabies centre is required so that the rabies vaccine can be administered. *Do not wait for symptoms as the disease is always fatal once symptoms develop.*

Apart from such serious considerations, any dog bite may go septic due to commonly occurring germs. All bites should be treated promptly with an antiseptic. (*See* ABRASION.) For severe bites, consult a doctor. Tetanus is another potentially fatal disease which can be acquired from a cut or dog bite. Everyone can be immunised against tetanus so that this problem need not arise. Check with your doctor that your immunity is up-to-date.

Dotage
(*See* OLD AGE.)

Double Vision (*Diplopia*)
Diplopia may be due to weakness or lack of balance of the eye muscles (*see* SQUINT). Occasionally it may be due to illness so anyone who sees double should consult a doctor urgently. Glasses or eye exercises may be all that are required, but if there is a serious cause the

sooner it is dealt with the better.

Drinking
(*See* ALCOHOLISM, ADDICTION, *and page 17.*)

Dropsy
(*See* OEDEMA.)

Drowning
Drowning occurs when enough oxygen cannot reach the lungs following submersion in water. Without a continual supply from the air the tissues of the body rapidly die. In drowning, therefore, it is vital to restore normal breathing if there is the slightest chance of recovery. **SEE ARTIFICIAL RESPIRATION, page 39.**

Drug
Any substance which affects the working of the body, and is used in treatment. The term is *not* restricted to substances which cause drowsiness or addiction.

Drug Addiction and Abuse
In all types of drug addiction the body becomes dependent on more and more quantities of drug with ever more damage from side effects. Young people should realise that there is nothing clever in getting involved in pot parties where even stronger drugs may be passed around. It is not certain whether the long term effects of pot are as medically damaging as those of alcohol or nicotine but it is certain that some untoward effects have been demonstrated with continued use and the risk is not worth taking. A danger in joining in group activities is of being introduced, perhaps accidentally, to a very disturbing drug such as LSD. This produces hallucinations (the 'trip') which can be nightmarish or euphoric. Unfortunately, during a euphoric sense of power people have jumped from buildings under the impression that they could fly. The

'low' trips can produce a nightmarish variety of depression which can persist for months after the original dose.

Another killer is heroin, often used with cocaine. Here the increasing physical dependence and complications may lead to death. Tragic mistakes occur as when a man foolishly injects his girl friend with a dose that he is taking, forgetting that he has worked his way up to what is a lethal dose for a newcomer.

Most dangerous of all is the risk of infection with the AIDS virus or Hepatitis B if needles are shared.

Some people seem to be more prone to addiction than others and can rapidly become hooked. No-one should get involved with even the mildest of pot smoking or pill swapping groups. You may be the unlucky one. Only foolish people run such risks, which can harm for life, or kill.

Duodenal Ulcer

The duodenum is part of the small intestine leading out of the stomach. An ulcer is a gap in the lining of the duodenum so that the sensitive underlayers are exposed. Due to imbalance in the digestive juices reaching the duodenum from the stomach, the lining becomes inflamed and later eroded to form an ulcer. Smoking, irregular, infrequent meals and mental stress predispose to ulcers.

A substance called histamine is important in controlling the acidity of stomach juice and its release is controlled by certain nerves. Nicotine and adrenalin (the 'stress hormone') affect histamine release. Several drugs are now available which block histamine release and allow ulcers to heal.

The progress of ulcers can be checked by barium X-rays and a flexible telescope (or endoscope) for direct viewing into the stomach.

Typical symptoms are pain which remains fairly localised a little above the naval. It comes on an hour or so after meals; it may last for the best part of an hour, sometimes with a feeling of sickness and occasionally vomiting. Flatulence (wind) is common. Ulcers require medical treatment, for if they continue there is a danger of internal bleeding or of the ulcer spreading through the wall and causing a perforation. Bed rest is still useful in severe cases. A special diet is not required but it is sensible to avoid any foods which cause symptoms. A patient will find items to be avoided by trial and error. The important point is regular, frequent meals. Alkali tablets may help. The mainstay of treatment however is the newer type 'healing tablet' combined with *giving up smoking* and avoiding stress.

If the ulcer will not heal, and pain is severe, an operation may be needed such as a vagotomy which cuts the nerves to the stomach. Normally this presents no difficulties in skilled hands.

Dysentery
Infectious disease of the intestines caused by bacteria which give rise to inflammation. The germs are spread by contaminated food and water supplies, etc. The disease is rare in the UK but common in hot climates. Symptoms are diarrhoea, which may be accompanied by a little blood, colicky pain in the stomach and usually fever. Attention to fluid requirements, bowel slowing tablets, and appropriate antibiotics will usually cut short an attack. See your doctor.

Another type of dysentery found in Asia and the Tropics is caused by a parasite which burrows in the wall of the intestine. This is known as *amoebic dysentery*, and although the symptoms are usually less severe it runs a more chronic course than bacterial dysentery and may present with constipation. Travellers from Asia and the Tropics with persistent bowel symptoms need specialised investigation.

Dyslexia

'Word blindness' – in which a person of normal intelligence has difficulty in learning to read. In UK sufferers can be referred to special centres.

Dysmenorrhoea

Painful periods can be due to many causes. They are most common in girls between the ages of 15 and 25. Girls with severe pain often produce high levels of substances called Prostaglandins which cause muscle spasms in the womb. If the pain is not relieved by simple painkillers, your doctor can prescribe other treatments. Painful periods in middle age or at other times may be due to other gynaecological disorders. If they persist consult your doctor.

Dyspareunia

The term given to painful sexual intercourse. In the woman there is usually some difficulty the first time intercourse takes place. The entrance to the vagina (female passage) is more or less sealed by a membrane known as the hymen, and this must be broken before full penetration can take place. Sometimes where early attempts have been clumsy or painful the woman becomes frightened or apprehensive so that subsequent union is difficult for her and her partner. Girls who dreamed intercourse would be fabulous (it can be but not at first) often find the required adjustments a bit of a shock. If the man is patient, encouraging and above all loving, and gives his girl time, perhaps even days, before entering *fully*, normally all should come right within weeks.

In some cases dyspareunia is due to disease or inflammation of the vagina or pelvic organs. Where dyspareunia comes on suddenly after previously painless intercourse, medical investigation is needed. A few marriages are doomed because the couples are, for one reason or another, unable to establish a proper physical union, and it is vital that advice should be sought if there is continued difficulty. (*See* FRIGIDITY.)

Dyspepsia
A rather loose term covering different types of indigestion. Dyspepsia usually implies discomfort and flatulence following meals. It may be due to over-indulgence (*see* ACIDOSIS) or at other times associated with internal disorders, such as ulcers (*see* DUODENAL ULCER) or gallstones.

E

Earache

May be due to several causes such as infection of the middle ear (*see* OTITIS MEDIA) which may follow a cold. Small boils known as furuncles sometimes develop in the canal leading from the outer ear to the ear drum and are very painful. They require medical advice.

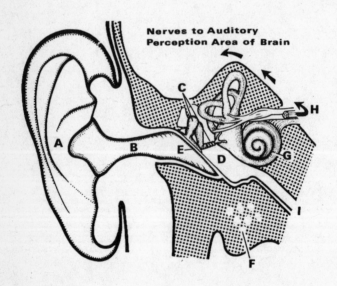

Fig. 6 The ear

A	Auricle	F	Mastoid process containing air cells
B	Canal leading to ear drum		
C	Ossicles	G	Cochlea
D	Cavity of middle ear	H	Auditory nerve
E	Ear drum	I	Eustachian tube

The amount of wax produced varies from person to person but is sometimes sufficient to block the ear completely and causes discomfort. When this happens it may be removed by a doctor or nurse using a syringe. The wax should be softened with almond oil or Waxsol for a few days first. Earache is often a great worry in children and, if it does not quickly settle down or if it is associated with any fever, the child should always be seen by a doctor. Antibiotics may be needed and careful follow-up by the doctor is necessary to prevent complications like deafness and mastoiditis. For temporary relief, Paracetamol and warmed ear drops of 'Audax' or 'Auralgicin' are helpful.

Temporary earache can afflict airline passengers. When the aircraft ascends, passengers may notice their ears 'popping', but this does not result in pain.

When an aircraft descends, the pressure in the cabin increases and the eardrums are pushed inwards, which can produce pain. The remedy is to 'clear the ears', which is achieved by yawning, swallowing, chewing, sucking, wiggling the jaw, or by closing the mouth and blowing against a nose which is pinched firmly shut. Babies can be helped by being given a drink.

It is unwise to fly with nasal congestion (e.g. cold or hay fever, etc.), and those who suffer should consult a doctor, as should anyone whose discomfort persists more than a few hours after landing. (*See* DEAFNESS, MASTOID *and* OTORRHOEA.)

Echo-Cardiography
The use of echo-recording in the diagnosis of cardiac conditions.

Ectopic Pregnancy
A pregnancy which occurs outside the womb. The womb is connected by means of two tubes with the ovaries. The female egg or ovum passes down these tubes (the Fallopian tubes) into the womb and when

fertilisation takes place the ovum normally lodges in the uterus. It occasionally happens that the fertilised ovum lodges in one of the tubes. When this occurs there is no room for the ovum to grow, so that trouble soon develops. Often there is pain in the lower part of the abdomen on one side and brown discharge or slight bleeding from the vagina. If the condition continues the Fallopian tube may burst. The symptoms often occur soon after a missed period before pregnancy is confirmed so in the event of pain and brown discharge contact your doctor without delay even if you are not sure you are pregnant. The treatment of an ectopic pregnancy is by operation to remove the bursting tube. Both ovaries and one healthy tube are left, so fertility is not greatly affected.

Eczema

A chronic skin disease in which the most prominent features are redness, soreness, weeping and irritation. It is often seen over the knuckles, wrists and elbows, and may be associated with widespread dryness and scaling of the skin. The condition is due to sensitivity of the skin (*see* ALLERGY) and similar conditions such as asthma or hay fever may be met with in the same family.

Eczema is common in babies (infantile eczema), and sometimes food allergies may be found responsible. The 'foreign' protein in cow's milk can cause allergy in babies and may even be responsible for long term problems. Breast feeding largely avoids this problem and if there is a family history of allergy, cow's milk should not be given during the first six months of life if possible. Fortunately many babies will grow out of the tendency to develop eczema. The treatment of *established* eczema is difficult, and often calls for perseverance in the doctor and patient as the condition may be due to 'atopy' (atopic with dry skin/eczema). Cotton clothes should be worn and overheating avoided.

Eczema patients should never use soap. Oily preparations such as oilatum can be used for washing. Various types of cream and ointment can be prescribed by your doctor. Treatment has to be continued as long as the eczema persists. At all times chemical irritants should be avoided.

Electric Shock
The danger from the passage of electricity through the body is threefold. Firstly, there may be a burn at the points where the electric current enters and leaves. This may be treated on general lines. (*See* BURNS.) Secondly, the current has a paralysing effect on the nervous system and the heart. The victim may be stunned into unconsciousness and the heart may stop beating and breathing may cease. Thirdly, strong muscular spasms are provoked which are damaging and may lead to temporary paralysis and stiffness.

When a person suffers electric shock, first make certain that contact with the current is broken. Do not touch the victim with your hand or you will suffer a shock yourself, but use some non-conducting material, a stick, a wooden chair, a cushion – something dry and *not* containing metal. Next, see if the victim is breathing. If he is, he may be kept warm and made comfortable, but if not, apply artificial respiration until medical help arrives. If you suspect that the heart has stopped (confirm by ear directly over the left nipple area), a sharp blow of the fist directly over the breast bone (centre of the chest) will occasionally re-start it. (*See* ARTIFICIAL RESPIRATION *page 39.*)

Electric shocks are best prevented, and great care with switches, etc., especially in *bathrooms* (for water acts as a conductor) is recommended. 'Pull' switches should always be used for electric lights in bathrooms. Electric fires should never be used there, except for the high wall-fitted types with pull switches.

Great care should be taken in the kitchen so that

damp hands are never used to deal with switches and plugs. 'Safety' wall sockets should always be used, especially where there are children in the house. All electrical gadgets should be checked by an expert at the slightest sign of defects, and house wiring should meet modern safety standards; improvements should be undertaken by qualified electricians only.

Electrocardiograph/Electrocardiogram (*ECG*)

Electrical tracing of heart activity which alters in heart disease and is useful in detecting certain types of cardiac illness e.g. coronary thrombosis.

Electro Convulsive Therapy (*ECT*)

The passage of a tiny electric current through the brain in carefully measured doses to help serious depressive illness and some forms of schizophrenia. This would normally induce convulsions but the patients are given muscle relaxants to prevent this. Although there is much controversy about its use on the grounds that permanent physical damage may be done, it seems to be life-saving in severe depression where other treatments have failed; in these cases there is a high risk of suicide as the patient's feelings of misery are so great that life does not seem worth living. There is usually some memory loss immediately after treatment but this improves with time. I have known many who have had this treatment years ago and they now seem perfectly well. (*See* MENTAL ILLNESS.)

Electroencephalogram (*EEG*)

Electrical tracing of the 'brain waves', helpful in confirming the diagnosis of epilepsy and other brain diseases.

Embolism

A clot of blood or other particle carried round the blood stream may lodge in a blood vessel and block it.

This cuts off the blood supply to the organ in question, causing tissue damage. Thus a cerebral embolism is a blood clot lodged in one of the arteries of the brain and is one cause of a stroke. (*See* STROKE.) Sometimes the clot can be dispersed by urgent medical treatment with anti-coagulant tablets and/or surgical removal of the clot.

Emphysema
Swelling and bursting of the delicate terminal air passages in the lungs. It is often associated with narrowing of the large air tubes (bronchi) due to chronic bronchitis. The passage of oxygen into the blood is less effective than it should be and extreme shortness of breath results.

Empyema
An empyema can be described as an abscess on the lung (*see* ABSCESS). The lung is enclosed in a double layer of membrane which protects it, and, if the lung becomes inflamed, fluid may form between the layers. If germs spread from the lung, this fluid may become infected and an empyema has developed. This may happen following pneumonia but nowadays antibiotics generally clear a chest infection before this stage. If pus does collect, it may be drained by a tube inserted into the chest.

Encephalitis
The medical term for inflammation of the brain; a serious condition due to infection by germs – usually the small germs known as viruses. It may occur alone or as a complication of a general illness such as measles; this is one good reason for immunisation against the disease in the second year of life (the risk of encephalitis from the vaccine is much smaller than that from the disease itself). The patient with encephalitis is seriously ill, and may be unconscious or delirious. The outlook

for permanent recovery is fairly good.

Endometriosis
One cause of painful periods. In this condition the menstrual flow tends to run backwards so that fragments of the shed womb lining reach the Fallopian tubes and the ovaries, rather than being completely voided into the vagina. One type of ovarian cyst may form (chocolate cyst) and resultant abdominal pain and possible infertility require medical attention. Treatment is by hormones and by removal of the cysts. (*See* DYSMENORRHOEA *and* OVARIAN CYST.)

Enuresis (*Bed wetting*)
A troublesome and common complaint in children. The age a child gains control of the bladder varies considerably; but by the age of four night control is generally achieved. The child only gains voluntary control of his bladder around eighteen months and the ability to use the toilet alone around two to two-and-a-half years. Although regular 'potting' of a baby before this age may save wet nappies this is not 'training' as no true bladder control is involved. The main help that a mother can give the eighteen month child is to offer the pot after meals, on coming indoors, after walking, etc., but to abandon the attempt after two minutes if there is no response. She should be ready to produce the pot and help the child onto it if he indicates his need but she must also be philosophically prepared for a lot of refusals, false alarms and general messing about. When day-time control is achieved, 'potting' the child last thing at night may induce night-time dryness. By two-and-a-half the child may co-operate in using a bedside potty, when the night nappy may be discarded. It should not be left off too soon as 'accidents' discourage the child and make matters worse. The child will always gain bladder control day and night in his own good time provided that he is given a chance to do so and that he

108

has no undue emotional upsets.

If a child of four is constantly wetting the bed, ask your doctor to check his water in case infection is the cause. Usually there is no abnormality and the child gains control a little later. Persistent 'dribbling' as opposed to a series of small floods, always requires urgent medical investigation.

Some families seem to have 'immature' bladders in that many members gain night control very late in childhood. Most doctors will offer treatment at four-and-a-half to five years. Undue restriction of fluids is not helpful and can be cruel. Children may temporarily start wetting the bed again (after being dry) during a family upheaval or hospital admission. Reassurance (and not scolding) is required. (*See* INCONTINENCE.)

Epilepsy

A disease in which the patient suffers from recurrent fits. It appears to be due to inherent electrical instability in the brain, so that every so often there is a sudden release of energy. The instability may be caused by head injury or disease. But often there is no obvious reason and this type of epilepsy begins early in life and tends to run in families. There are many types of epilepsy. In childhood the commonest is absences (called *petit mal*) in which lapses of consciousness lasting only a few seconds occur. These may be very frequent and scarcely noticeable to the onlooker. They are important as a reason for poor progress or apparent inattentiveness at school. EEG (*see page 106*) helps confirm the diagnosis and fortunately the majority of children grow out of them.

Children may also have tonic-clonic fits (major fits or *grand mal*) which is the commonest form in adults. Often the patient has warning before this type of fit occurs. He sees flashes of light, or may experience some peculiar sensations, known as the aura. Following this there is often a cry and the patient falls unconscious. The body is stiff and rigid, but after a short while rapid jerking movements occur which gradually diminish. The patient goes blue in the face, and may bite his tongue or pass water. During the fit it is best to do as little as possible. If the patient can be caught as he falls, injury may be prevented. He should be allowed to lie flat until the fit is over; the neck should be examined to see that it is not constricted by tight clothing. After the fit the patient should be put to bed, and he will often sleep. This type of seizure is similar to the feverish convulsion in childhood. (*See* CONVULSION.)

A doctor must be called at the onset of any convulsion in children so that he can, if necessary, give an injection to stop it; prolonged fits can be dangerous. Most adults come out of a fit spontaneously but medical aid must be sought if it persists more than ten minutes. Anticonvulsive medicines can bring about a great reduction in frequency of fits, or even eliminate them. An epileptic may hold a driving licence if he has not had a daytime fit for two years. A heavy goods vehicle licence can never be granted to anyone with a history of even one fit (other than infantile feverish convulsions).

In general, epileptics should lead as full a life as possible, but they must avoid occupations in which a fit would prove dangerous such as flying, driving, window cleaning, scaffolding or proximity to moving machinery. Ill-informed prejudice against epileptics by employers is to be deprecated. Many doctors have controlled epilepsy themselves. Guidance may be had from the British Epilepsy Association (ask your doctor for the address).

Episiotomy
Small cut sometimes made under local anaesthetic at the outlet of the vagina, to aid delivery of the baby's head during birth. It avoids overstretching of the muscles and prevents a larger tear; it is stitched up painlessly under local anaesthetic.

Erysipelas

A spreading skin infection similar to cellulitis (*see* CELLULITIS). In erysipelas, however, the streptococcal infection spreads within the skin instead of just beneath. The treatment is penicillin.

Erythema

Redness of the skin, a feature of many rashes and children's illnesses.

Euthanasia

Means easy or happy death. There are well-meaning people who feel that the individual should be granted the right when incurably ill to ask for release from life at the stage he deems appropriate. The means envisaged is usually a painless injection of a lethal dose of opiate or similar. Euthanasia is illegal.

Strangely, the idea is more popular with younger healthy people who witness what they see as the disintegration and degradation of a person they once loved. The patient himself, although perhaps a believer in euthanasia, rarely seems to feel that the 'right' moment has come. Hospices such as St Christopher's have brought hope of a pain-free and a fulfilling life to the incurably ill. These patients live every day to the full and accept death on its own terms.

Eyes (Eyesight)

Care of the eyes is important. Inflammation may be due to many causes. Eyes becoming red and irritable, particularly towards the end of the day, are probably being strained. Possibly there may be a slight irregularity in the lens which makes the focusing of light on the back of the eye difficult. The lens may be too flat, which makes the focusing of distant objects easy, but near vision difficult – the condition of long sightedness or *hypermetropia*. If the lens is too curved there is *myopia* or short sightedness; while if the lens is

1. Normal Vision
The light from an outside object is brought to a focus accurately on the sensitive retina at the back of the eyeball.

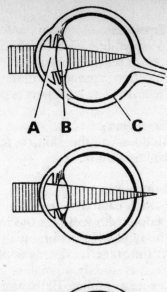

2. Hypermetropia
(Long sightedness)
The eyeball is too short or the lens is too weak, so that the light comes to a focus *behind* the retina. Distant objects can be seen more clearly than near ones. Convex glasses are required to correct this error.

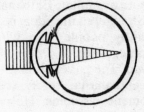

3. Myopia
(Short sightedness)
The eyeball is too long or the lens is too powerful, so that the light comes to a focus *in front of* the retina. Near objects can be seen more clearly than distant ones. Concave glasses are required to correct this error.

4. Astigmatism
Either the eyeball or the lens is irregular so that light is brought to a focus at different levels in different parts of the eye. Special glasses have to be made to correct the individual error in astigmatism.

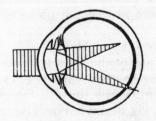

Fig. 7 Defective vision
A   Pupil
B   Lens
C   Retina

irregular, being too curved in one direction and too flat in another, the condition is described as *astigmatism*. All require glasses or contact lenses.

Various germs can set up inflammation and discharge in the lining of the eye – known as *conjunctivitis* (*see* CONJUNCTIVITIS). If the inflammation does not subside quickly a doctor should be consulted.

Strong sunlight can also cause inflammation in susceptible people, and the eyes should be protected by dark (polarised lens) glasses during the summer, especially at the seaside where the glare can be strong. Misuse of an ultraviolet (sunlight) lamp can cause severe inflammation. Always use the goggles provided and follow the time exposure instructions minutely.

Another cause of irritation is a small particle lodging in the eye. The eye containing a 'foreign body' should on no account be rubbed, as this may damage the delicate membrane. The lids should be held open and the eye carefully inspected – under the top lid with the patient looking down, and under the lower lid while looking up. If the particle can be seen, it should be gently removed with a wisp of cotton wool or the corner of a clean soft handkerchief. Sometimes gently pulling the upper lid over the lower will remove the particle. Often holding the head over a basin of clean water, opening and closing the eye lids under the water can get rid of a particle in the eye. If the particle cannot be seen or moved, the patient should be taken to the doctor.

At times the ducts may be blocked causing watery eyes. These can sometimes be cleared by a doctor in a minute or two.

Two important causes of *painful* red eyes are *glaucoma* (*see* GLAUCOMA) and inflammation of the iris (*see* IRITIS). Among warning signs in glaucoma are episodes of mistiness of vision and haloes round lights. These or *any type of sudden visual disturbance indicate the need for urgent investigation*.

Most people probably need glasses around 50. It is

unwise to delay being tested if any difficulties are experienced; thereafter have eyesight professionally checked as required, probably every two years.

A doctor should be seen for any pain, sticky discharge, disturbance of vision or persistently red or watery eyes. (*See* ARTERITIS, CATARACT *and* PINK EYE.)

Short sight (myopia), which causes difficulty in seeing objects clearly in the distance, usually requires the wearing of glasses or contact lenses. Recently a laser operation to correct the vision has become available (see your doctor).

F

Fainting
A momentary loss of consciousness for which there are many causes. Most faints are not serious and quickly pass. Their cause is often emotional. Some people faint at the sight of blood, others in church or on receiving bad news. These factors cause a temporary upset in the nervous control of the circulation which results in the faint. People vary in their make-up, and some go through life without fainting, while others faint readily. It can be much reduced by the advice to wiggle the toes continuously – thus aiding blood return from the legs to the heart. The person who faints should be kept flat. Nothing more is required, and *it is unwise to try to force fluids (brandy, etc.) down the throat, as this may cause choking*. For a *feeling* of faintness sit and put the head between the knees as far down as possible until the feeling passes.

In a few cases fainting may be a symptom of illnesses such as *anaemia* or occasionally heart disease. In general a single faint, particularly where there is some emotional cause or in heat, should not be cause for alarm. If, however, a patient faints repeatedly and apparently without reason a doctor must be consulted to see if there is any underlying cause.

Festering
(*See* ABSCESS.)

Fever
The temperature of the human body is carefully

115

regulated, and under normal circumstances varies little. It is normally about 98° Fahrenheit or 37° Centigrade and should not exceed 98.4°F. When the body is attacked by germs a complicated defence system comes into play, and one of the body's reactions is to increase temperature. This serves two purposes. Firstly, the raised temperature is often unsuitable for germs so that they can be more easily destroyed, and, secondly, as the temperature is raised the internal workings of the body are speeded up so that it can work more quickly and efficiently. However, the temperature is only one of many factors to be taken into account and the patient's appearance and other symptoms must be considered. Children 'run a temperature' more easily than adults and a mother may be surprised to find that a child with a head cold, not looking particularly ill, has a temperature of 100°F or so. This can be readily treated at home with Paracetamol unless complications such as earache or chest symptoms occur.

On the other hand, a temperature of only 99° to 100°F may be very significant in a patient who feels very unwell, especially if there is abdominal pain or vomiting.

As a general rule you need medical advice for a child who has a temperature of 102°F (39°C) and for an adult with a temperature of over 100°F (38°C) but again it is the severity of the symptoms which matters. If your child looks ill, and flushed, is not eating, is complaining of pain or is vomiting you need medical advice regardless of the reading on the thermometer. (*See* HYPOTHERMIA *and* TEMPERATURE.)

Fibroids
Small lumps which develop in the wall of the uterus (womb). They become increasingly common in middle age. Usually the chief symptom is increased loss – 'flooding' at the 'period'. If symptomless they can be left alone but if flooding is severe drugs or hysterectomy

may be the best treatment (*see* HYSTERECTOMY). Surprisingly, removal of fibroids from the uterus is a more difficult operation than hysterectomy and is only done in women who wish to have further children especially if the fibroids may be causing infertility. Fibroids are not dangerous in themselves, and are not malignant.

Fibrositis
(*See* MUSCULAR RHEUMATISM.)

Filariasis (Elephantiasis)
A tropical disease caused by a filaria worm carried by mosquitoes. It causes swellings of the glands and skin so that enormously swollen legs appear.

Finger, Septic
Infection by germs in the soft tissues of the finger is common and can lead to disability if not treated. It may follow a prick or injury, but often the breach in the skin is so small as to escape notice. The finger becomes red, swollen, hot and throbs. Treatment with hot poultices and antibiotics should be started as early as possible. The finger should always be protected and the arm rested in a sling. It is always best to consult a doctor for any infection of the finger. If the infection spreads to the base of the nail it will often become chronic and may fail to clear up until the nail is removed. A further danger is that the infection may spread to the tendons which move the finger joints. If this happens, the finger may remain permanently stiff.

Fissure-in-Ano
The opening from the 'back passage' is guarded by a circular muscle – the anus. A small split can develop in the overlying skin as a split may develop at the corner of the mouth. This is known as a fissure-in-ano. There is sharp pain each time the bowels are opened, and there may be bleeding. Infection by germs and the fact

that the anus is stretched when the bowels are opened make healing difficult. It may respond to keeping the motions soft by a laxative and to an anaesthetic cream prescribed by your doctor. A small operation may be needed to restore to normal. This condition can often be prevented by avoiding constipation. (*See* CONSTI-PATION.)

Fistula

An abnormal opening between internal organs or between an organ and the surface of the body. A common type is the fistula-in-ano due to infection deep in a fissure-in-ano (see previous article). Treatment is by a minor operation. Pus collects to form an abscess (*see* ABSCESS) and this bursts on to the skin surface close by but *not through* the original fissure. This 'abscess' thus has two openings and constitutes a fistula.

Fits

(*See* CONVULSION *and* EPILEPSY.)

Flat Foot

The foot has to support the weight of the body for long periods and put up with tremendous stresses during walking, etc. It is constructed on the principle of the arch. There are really two arches formed by the bones of the foot: the longitudinal arch running from front to back; and the transverse arch running from side to side. The bones are kept in place by the muscles, tendons and ligaments which bind them together. In 'flat foot', the arch sags so that the inner side of the foot touches the ground. It is so common in children that specialists now consider this to be one variety of normal. The foot is painless, arches normally on tiptoe and does not need special exercise or footwear. Where flat foot is painful and caused by arthritis or other diseases orthopaedic help is needed.

Flatulence
The escape of wind from the digestive tract. The term is usually applied to eructations from the stomach ('belching') but is also used to describe wind from the bowels. Excessive flatulence may be a symptom of disordered digestion (*see* DYSPEPSIA) and is sometimes associated with gall bladder disease or peptic ulcer.

Flooding (*See* MENORRHAGIA.)

Flushing (*See* MENOPAUSE.)

Food Poisoning
There are two sorts. In the first the food may be poisonous, for example, when poisonous fungus is eaten by mistake. In the second the food is innocent, but is invaded by germs such as salmonella and e.coli and goes bad; and it is the poison produced by the germs which is responsible for the symptoms. Tinned foods opened and left standing are particularly liable to 'go off'. The body usually makes every endeavour to get rid of the poison, and severe abdominal pain is followed by vomiting. At a later stage there is usually diarrhoea. Unidentified foods should never be eaten, and one should be suspicious of mushrooms gathered by anyone but an expert. With regard to household foods, if there is suspicion as to their wholesomeness they are better discarded. This particularly applies to shellfish such as mussels and oysters. Better waste than a serious (occasionally fatal) illness. Tinned foods which have been partly used, and foods cooked and left standing, particularly in hot weather, should be suspect. Frozen poultry should be completely thawed before cooking and cooked food intended for fridge or freezer should be stored as soon as it has cooled to room temperature – not left lying around in a warm state – an ideal incubator for germs. Be very suspicious and careful of

119

any dented or bulging tins. If food poisoning is suspected, the remains of the meal should be preserved, and medical help summoned. The patient is best in bed and kept warm.

Fracture *(Broken Bone)*
The treatment of this falls outside our scope. For those unskilled in first aid the guiding rule with fractures should be to do as little as possible. To move the injured part will often cause further damage. The victim should be made comfortable, kept warm, treated for shock (*see* SHOCK), and the injured part given some support (with as little movement as possible) until medical help arrives.

Freckles
Freckles are sometimes a cause of annoyance. There is no effective treatment and if you have the type of skin which pigments in patches instead of all over, as far as possible avoid exposure to the sun.

Frequency of Urination
Very common. Several causes are dealt with under various illnesses but frequency is sometimes only a symptom of worry, cold, excessive drinking and occasionally follows prolonged love-making. In such instances, the cure is to remove the cause. It does not normally help to reduce fluids except perhaps to abandon late night tea or more especially coffee. Individuals vary greatly in frequency. (*See* CYSTITIS, INSOMNIA, KIDNEY DISEASES, PREGNANCY, PROSTATE, PYELONEPHRITIS, RETENTION OF URINE.)

Frigidity
Sexual coldness in the female. It varies from mild indifference to refusal or inability to allow intercourse. The latter type in which penetration is impossible may occur in a woman the first time she has a sex

relationship. There may be conditions in the woman or her mate where some physical trouble is the cause; a thick hymen, for example, may need a small operation. These rare instances require prompt advice from the family doctor. They should be curable.

Almost all frigidity is based on fear, guilt feelings or ignorance, and happily can usually be conquered with understanding and love – the great aphrodisiac which performs miracles.

All differ in sex needs; some want a lot, others little. Variety in preliminary love play and positions helps to prevent boredom. Men often fail to appreciate that most women need to be cuddled and some, intimately kissed, if they are to be turned fully on before intercourse. There are many books available giving advice on sexual techniques.

For any serious difficulty – and they do happen or may develop – visit your doctor or seek advice from a trained counsellor.

Frost Bite *and* **Cold Extremities**
Tissue damage caused by cold. Frost bite develops in the extremities after exposure. A finger, toe, etc., becomes waxy in appearance and is usually seen in subjects (e,g, mountaineers) who have been exposed to sub-zero temperatures. Treatment is by gradual warming under medical supervision as gangrene (tissue death) is a great risk. The more common painful or numb fingers, especially in the elderly, in everyday cold conditions are best avoided by wearing several layers of warm clothing, avoiding tight garments on the limbs and having regular warm meals. A part which has become numb should be warmed *very* gradually. Here a warm drink is very effective and active rubbing should be avoided. *Trying to help by using hot water can cause excruciating agony, so do not do so*. (*See* RAYNAUD'S DISEASE, CHILBLAIN.)

G

Gall Bladder (*Gall Stones*)
A small hollow pouch attached to the liver. (*See Fig. 1, page 35.*) It receives bile made by the liver, and pours this into the duodenum where it aids digestion. The gall bladder is sometimes attacked by germs, and becomes inflamed – a condition known as *Cholecystitis*. In some cases, stones form within the gall bladder, and they may cause pain, and can be associated with flatulence and indigestion. Suspected gall stones can usually be seen on X-ray and if present they are often best removed by operation along with the gall bladder. The patient usually recovers well. Small gall stones can be dissolved by drugs but this takes several months and many recur.

Ganglion
A type of cyst in the lining of a tendon often occurring near the wrist. It may cause discomfort but is harmless and often disappears spontaneously in six to twelve months. If it is persistent a minor operation will cure.

Gangrene
A condition in which a part of the body dies. It is usually due to interference with circulation and may result from a blood clot in the vessel supplying the part (*see* EMBOLISM); or it may be due to progressive narrowing of the blood vessels which keep the part alive. This type of gangrene is not uncommon in the aged, and usually attacks the toe which becomes blackened and shrivels. Elderly people and diabetics

should have regular chiropody as small cuts on the feet can precipitate serious trouble.

Gas Poisoning
Caused by the carbon monoxide content of coal gas. England, Wales and Scotland, as well as many other parts of the world are on *Natural Gas* (methane-based) which is not poisonous, but gas poisoning may be possible in other parts of the world where coal gas is still used and anywhere where appliances may be faulty. (*See* ARTIFICIAL RESPIRATION, ASPHYXIA.)

Gastric Ulcer
The article on DUODENAL ULCER should be consulted. It is a similar condition arising in the stomach. The pain following meals comes on earlier than in duodenal ulcer – usually in about half an hour, but apart from this the symptoms differ little, and the treatment is similar. Operation is more often advisable for this type of ulcer as there is a risk of malignancy (cancer).

Gastritis
Inflammation of the stomach, it may follow excessive alcohol or food poisoning. The term is often used for indigestion. (*See* ACIDOSIS *and* DYSPEPSIA.)

General Paralysis of the Insane (*GPI*)
(*See* SYPHILIS.)

Genes
Inherited constitutents of chromosomes within every living cell, the genes are molecular arrangements of DNA and the patterns are inherited from both parents. When a defective gene occurs, it produces conditions such as Down's Syndrome (mongolism) or muscular dystrophy. Research into this type of disorder may lead to prevention and, through gene therapy, removal of the disorder.

German Measles (*Rubella*)

One of the acute infectious childhood illnesses; most children catch it, usually during school years. As with the other illnesses of this nature a second attack is uncommon. The disease is spread by contact between children, and often occurs in epidemics. The incubation period (the time between contact and the development of symptoms) is generally two to three weeks. The rash is usually the first sign. This consists of flat pink spots which may merge together after one or two days. The glands at the back of the neck are enlarged and tender. Slight fever and 'cold' like symptoms may occur. The rash usually fades after about three days, and may be followed by slight peeling. German measles is not a serious disease and complications are rare.

The patient is infectious for five days after the rash appears. If an expectant mother within the first three months of pregnancy, who has not previously had the disease, comes into contact with it, she should consult a doctor as soon as possible. This is because there is a risk of the unborn baby's development being affected, if the mother contracts the disease.

There is no point in keeping children away from German measles sufferers as it it desirable that they should catch this mild illness and acquire immunity. For some years, immunisation has been offered to all girls in the UK at about 11 years. In October 1988 a new combined Measles, Mumps and Rubella vaccine was introduced and is now offered to all children during their second year. Adult women who are not immune should contact their GP or Local Authority clinic for information. It is imperative that they do not become pregnant within three months of being vaccinated, or be vaccinated while pregnant.

Germs (*Bacteria, viruses, etc.*)

Name given to small living organisms capable of invading the body and causing disease. Bacteria are measured in microns, each micron being 1/2500th of an inch. There are many types of bacteria, for instance, the staphylococcus which causes boils and the streptococcus which causes tonsillitis. Even smaller are the viruses which cause many illnesses including the common cold and influenza; they can be seen only with a powerful electron microscope.

Giddiness

The ear is also an organ of balance; there is a special part of the inner ear which helps to maintain our equilibrium. When this is upset we have a sensation of outside objects moving around, and this can occur when the inner ear is over-stimulated by rapid turning (e.g. on a piano stool). Sometimes this part of the ear may be irritated by disease, and true giddiness (vertigo) may result. Tablets can be prescribed to help. Some patients really mean a feeling of faintness when they talk of giddiness. (*See* FAINTING *and* TINNITUS.)

Glands

There are two different structures in the body referred to as glands. The unqualified term glands usually refers to the lymphatic glands, which are about the size of a pea and are distributed over the body. One of their functions is to filter out the poisons which are liberated when germs invade the body, and when this happens the glands often swell. Thus when germs invade the throat the glands in the neck will often swell up; and with a septic finger, for instance, a swollen gland may often be felt near the elbow.

The other types of gland produce substances which regulate the body's functions. If the gland has a channel or duct down which these substances pass it is known as an exocrine gland. Examples are sweat glands in the skin and the glands producing saliva which reaches the mouth by way of salivary ducts.

If a gland does not have a duct but pours its

secretions directly into the bloodstream it is known as a ductless or endocrine gland and the secretion as a HORMONE. Examples are the thyroid, ovary or testicle.

Glandular Fever (*Infective Mono-Nucleosis*)

An infective illness, caused by a virus. It commonly attacks children, adolescents and a few adults. The chief symptoms are sore throat and enlargement of the lymphatic glands, often throughout the body (*see* GLANDS). The disease is accompanied by fever, and occasionally a mild rash. The condition often lasts for several weeks, but although very unpleasant in the early days is not usually dangerous, and complications are uncommon. Rest is advisable during the feverish stage when the spleen may be enlarged and tender. Tiredness can persist, up to three months. Antibiotics do not help and treatment is by rest. Aspirin and Paracetamol may be taken to reduce fever and sore throat.

Glaucoma

Increased pressure inside the eyeball which if neglected can lead to blindness. It may be acute or chronic.

Acute glaucoma may be heralded by transient mistiness of vision and haloes round lights. Any disturbance of vision should be cause for immediate medical investigation as early glaucoma can usually be contained by prescription or appropriate eye drops, before the stage of permanent damage is reached.

Chronic glaucoma is more insidious and detected by pressure measurement of the eye by your optician or eye specialist.

Both types are helped by a small operation to aid drainage of fluid from the eye.

Gluten

The protein in wheat and other grain. Allergy to this produces coeliac disease in which the lining of the intestine becomes damaged so that food cannot be absorbed and malnutrition results. Treatment is by a gluten-free diet. (*See* SPRUE.)

Glycosuria
The term for sugar in the urine. The usual cause is diabetes. It may also occur in pregnancy.

Goitre
An enlarged thyroid gland. The thyroid is situated in the front of the neck, either side of the windpipe, and manufactures thyroxine, a hormone, which it pours into the blood. Thyroxine controls the speed at which the body works. With excess the body speeds up – the heart beats faster, weight is lost, etc.; with a lack it slows down. An enlarged thyroid gland may be associated with either too much or too little thyroxine. If there is too much, the goitre is said to be 'toxic' or the condition may be spoken of as *thyrotoxicosis*. If there is too little, the patient is always tired, the body becomes fat and sluggish and the condition is known as *myxoedema*. For a toxic goitre it may be necessary to operate and remove part of the gland, but sometimes operation can be avoided by using drugs which are capable of damping down the action of the thyroid. For the condition of myxoedema, it is necessary to give the patient thyroxine by mouth to restore the normal workings of the body. Sometimes goitre is due to a deficiency of iodine in the diet, and it tends to occur in areas where the water is lacking in iodine. Regular use of iodized salt (made by all leading salt manufacturers) can prevent this type of goitre. (*See* GLANDS, HORMONES.)

Gonorrhoea
One of the venereal diseases spread by sexual intercourse. It is due to a germ, the gonococcus, which invades the sex organs and sets up inflammation. In the male, symptoms usually commence about four days to a

week after intercourse, and there is sometimes some pain on passing water, and maybe yellowish discharge from the penis. In the female, the symptoms may be delayed and rather indefinite, but pain and some discharge from the vagina are usually present. The pain may seem worse on passing water and women may label this 'cystitis'. If a woman fears that her 'cystitis' could be due to a sexual contact, she should mention this to her doctor so that special tests can be made. Ordinary tests for 'cystitis' may miss gonorrhoea. Gonorrhoea can be rapidly cured by antibiotics, but treatment should be started early to ensure the best results.

Neglected gonorrhoea can have serious consequences. In the female it may spread and result in sterility or serious internal disorders, and in the male it may spread to affect the testicles (*see* ORCHITIS). Other unpleasant sequels to neglected gonorrhoea are acute arthritis (*see* ARTHRITIS), and the baby of an untreated mother may develop an infection of the eyes which leads to blindness.

It cannot be too strongly emphasised that if there are *any* symptoms suggestive of gonorrhoea a doctor should be consulted. If the disease is present treatment must be continued until tests show that cure is complete. Doctors at the special VD clinics arrange for sexual contacts to be traced and treated. As early symptoms in women may be nonexistent, a treated man can help his sexual partner (and perhaps many others) by informing her immediately of the risk. Rather a nasty shock now than subsequent abdominal abscesses or sterility later. As always, prevention is better than cure. The use of a sheath can prevent infection but is not foolproof. To neglect symptoms or to try to treat oneself by 'quack' remedies is to store up trouble for the future – not only for oneself but for others who may become infected. No need for shyness; doctors are not moralists and treatment is confidential. (*See* NSU.)

Gout

A form of painful arthritis caused by crystals of uric acid forming in the joints. The joint most often affected is at the base of the big toe, and the disease manifests itself by recurrent attacks of pain. Other joints can also be involved. Treatment consists briefly in moderation in drinking, reduction of offal in the diet, and in resting the joints during the acute attacks. Tablets can be used to lessen the joint inflammation during such attacks, and a drug called allopurinol taken regularly will prevent most recurrences as it reduces the level of uric acid in the body.

Guinea worm (*Dracontiasis*)

A tropical disease in which the worm goes under the skin and eventually protrudes through the skin. It is transmitted by a water shrimp (cyclops) in dirty water. The worm can be removed by winding it slowly round a stick over several days.

Gumma

(*See* SYPHILIS.)

H

Haematemesis

The vomiting of blood. The most common cause is the erosion of a blood vessel in the stomach by an ulcer or by the overfrequent use of aspirin (*see* GASTRIC *and* DUODENAL ULCER). Often the vomited blood retains its red colour, but sometimes it becomes altered by the gastric juice and assumes a dark brown colour. Anyone with a haematemesis should be put to bed and the doctor summoned urgently. Give nothing at all by mouth, but if thirst is complained of the patient may be given a little ice-cold water to sip. Patients should be treated in hospital where transfusion and other treatments can be used if bleeding continues. Sometimes an operation is advisable, but most cases recover without.

Haemophilia

A rare disease in which the blood fails to clot. Normally if a blood vessel is opened a complicated chemical action starts, which results in a part of the blood gradually becoming solid, and forming a clot. If this did not happen we should be liable to bleed to death from a small cut. In haemophilia a factor necessary for the clotting process is missing. The disease is congenital – i.e. one is born with it. It affects men only, but the condition is 'carried' by women who pass it on to their male children. Haemophiliacs can be treated by regular injections of the missing clotting factor.

Haemoptysis

The medial term for coughing up blood. The blood may be present as streaks in the sputum, is often bright red and may in some cases be frothy. There are many causes including minor chest and throat infections as well as heart disease, lung cancer and blood clot in the lung. Although tuberculosis is now uncommon in the West it is a cause of haemoptysis which is readily treated by modern drugs. Even a tiny haemoptysis should never be ignored. Chest X-rays and other investigations will facilitate accurate diagnosis and correct treatment.

Haemorrhage

The general term for bleeding. Internal haemorrhage is when bleeding occurs within the body, external when the blood escapes outside. Most bleeding is due to minor accidents and many people are unduly alarmed by the sight of blood. Recall the experience of thousands of blood donors who give a pint at a time, to see that a quantity of blood may be lost without harmful effects. For bleeding, such as cuts, the best treatment is to apply pressure to the part. This is best done by applying a clean handkerchief, gauze or cotton wool and bandaging firmly. The bleeding part should be raised – for example if the hand is bleeding the patient should lie on a bed with the hand resting on the head board. The dressing should not be disturbed as this may break up the clot, but if the bleeding continues a further firm bandage may be applied on top of the first. The use of a tourniquet is rarely necessary. Indeed sometimes it is dangerous, for a badly-applied tourniquet may increase bleeding.

Nose Bleeds (*Epistaxis*)

The best treatment is to sit over a wash basin with the head slightly forward, the mouth open, a cork between the teeth. The patient should breathe through the mouth and not swallow but allow the blood to run from the mouth. The nose should be squeezed firmly between finger and thumb and a cold pack placed on the bridge of the nose. The reason why nose bleeding often refuses to stop is because patients nearly always swallow the blood which trickles from the back of the nose. Each swallow moves the muscles of the mouth, and causes a tug on the blood vessel which dislodges the clot. By the measure described, the vessels remain undisturbed, so that a clot forms and the bleeding stops. Food and drink should be cool for the next twenty-four hours.

Haemorrhoids (*Piles*)
Small dilated blood vessels which occur in the region of the anus – the bowel exit, commonly known as *piles*. They are similar to varicose veins. They may cause irritation and some pain, or bleeding from the bowel particularly after the bowels have been opened. Sometimes also a pile 'comes down' and protrudes through the anus. Piles may respond to treatment with suppositories and cream twice daily for three weeks or less. The bowel action should be kept normal. Piles can also be treated by injection of a chemical which shrivels them up or by ligation (or banding). It may sometimes be necessary to remove them surgically or treat by dilatation of the anus under anaesthetic. The operation though uncomfortable in the early days is usually successful. Piles sometimes occur in pregnancy, due to increasing pressure caused by the growing child. These usually respond to conservative treatment and often disappear shortly after birth when the abdominal pressure returns to normal. *Haemorrhoids or anal discomfort which fails to respond to ten days' home treatment should be seen by a doctor.*

Hair
(*See* BALDNESS.)

132

Halitosis (*Bad Breath*)
This can occur with local disorders in the gums, teeth, throat or sinuses. It can also occur in distant diseases such as appendicitis, liver disease and diabetic coma as exhaled air contains odorous substances derived from the blood stream. If the cause is removed the trouble should go. Often a person is unduly sensitive about imagined offensiveness of breath. Treatment for anxiety rather than for halitosis may be required.

Hallucination
A condition in which something which does not exist is perceived. It may refer to any of the senses, so that hallucinations may be seen, felt or heard. They can occur in fever and delirium (*see* DELIRIUM) but are usually a symptom of mental illness e.g. schizophrenia or the result of drugs, e.g. LSD (*see* MENTAL ILLNESS). A hallucination is sometimes confused with a *delusion* which is wrong interpretation of something factual. A patient who looks at a blank wall and sees figures dancing is suffering from a hallucination. A man who hears his wife telephoning the butcher and becomes firmly convinced that she is arranging a meeting with her lover is suffering, probably, from a delusion.

Hammer Toe
A condition in which one of the toes, usually the second, becomes bent down at right angles. Protective felt pads over the toe prevent painful callosites. If pain persists the toe can be straightened by surgery. Often it is associated with bunion and is aggravated by wearing tight shoes. (*See* BURSA.)

Hare Lip
A deep split in the upper lip present at birth and due to a defect in development. It is curable by plastic surgery and cosmetic results are excellent. (*See* CLEFT PALATE.)

Hay Fever

An allergic disorder (*see* ALLERGY) in which there is an abnormal sensitivity to pollens. During the summer, trees, flowers and grasses produce thousands of pollen particles which are carried from plant to plant by the air. This pollen is not harmful but in a few who are sensitive it produces irritation of the nose and eyes. The hay fever season usually lasts from May to July, but varies according to which pollen is responsible for the symptoms. Much can be done to help. The newer antihistamine tablets such as Triludan relieve symptoms without causing drowsiness. Other treatments are available on prescription. Decongestant nose sprays should not be used for longer than 1 week. Desensitising injections are now rarely used.

Headache

A common complaint. Most have a simple explanation: worry, excessive drinking, overwork, hunger, smoking, too little sleep or a minor illness. Most of us suffer an occasional headache and this can usually be relieved by taking two aspirins or Paracetamols. Bathing the forehead with cold water sometimes brings relief but headaches often vanish as mysteriously as they arrive. When headaches become persistent notice must be taken, and some underlying cause sought. Eyestrain (*see* EYES) should be considered but contrary to popular belief does not often cause headaches. A headache on rising may lead to a suspicion of sinusitis (*see* ANTRUM). ANAEMIA is sometimes a cause, and stress may induce headaches. The majority of them are not serious, and not an indication of disease of the brain. If, however, headaches occur regularly or follow a bang on the head consult a doctor for advice.

Recurrent one-sided headaches (migraines) are common. These may be caused by caffeine, chocolate or alcohol and sometimes are brought on by strenuous exercise. Migraine can be disabling and, if frequent or

severe, medical advice should be sought. (*See* MIG-
RAINE.)

Heart and Heart Disease

The heart is a specially-adapted muscle, which pumps
the blood continuously round the body. The purpose of
this is to carry nourishment to the tissues, to take away
waste products from the tissues, and, perhaps most
important, to distribute oxygen from the air throughout
the body. Oxygen makes up about a fifth of the air we
breathe, and all living tissues need a constant supply.
Air is taken into the lungs where there is a meshwork of
tiny blood vessels, and the blood passing through
absorbs the oxygen we breathe in. This blood then
returns to the heart whence it is distributed via arteries
to the body. It returns to the heart after it has lost its
oxygen to the tissues, is pumped through the lungs
again to collect more oxygen, returns to the heart – and
so on. The heart is a four-chamber pump; two
chambers receiving blood (the atria) and two pumping
it out (the ventricles). It is also divided into two sides,
left and right, each consisting of one atrium and one
ventricle.

The heart may be affected in many ways. The muscle
may be damaged – sometimes by the poison from
germs, a condition known as *toxic myocarditis*. This
may follow various infectious illnesses; but fortunately
the damage is often temporary, and the heart muscle
recovers. *Rheumatic fever*, now fortunately rare in the
West, sometimes leaves permanent trouble behind, the
heart muscle being weakened and the heart valves
damaged. Sometimes, particularly later in life, the
muscle is weakened because too little blood reaches the
heart itself from the thickened coronary arteries. (*See*
ANGINA PECTORIS *and* CORONARY THROMBOSIS.)

In other cases the rhythm of the heart is disturbed.
Normally it beats steadily about 70 to 80 times a
minute, but sometimes due to disease the pumping

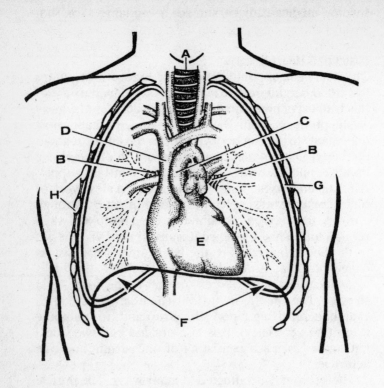

Fig. 8 The contents of the chest

A	Trachea, or windpipe	E	Heart
B	Bronchi	F	Diaphragm
C	Aorta	G	Double layer of pleura covering the lungs
D	Vena Cava	H	Ribs (cross section)

action becomes irregular, and less efficient.

The passage of blood through the heart is regulated by valves, which allow the blood to pass in one direction only. Sometimes these are affected by disease, so that they become too narrow, or inefficient, allowing blood to pass in the wrong direction. Nowadays valves can be successfully replaced by a synthetic model. This is of a course a major operation undertaken in specialised centres.

The heart muscle may be strained by having to cope with raised blood pressure but this is slow to develop and the condition is usually recognised before permanent harm is done.

Many drugs can be prescribed to help heart disease. You can help yourself by keeping your weight down, and giving up smoking. Walking is an excellent exercise and should be increased as far as advised. Worry is the worst enemy. Heart action, like digestion, is involuntary and best left to nature. The heart has a great reserve of power so that even when damaged it is able to cope with basic needs. No activities or interests should be given up unless they provide definite symptoms. Be guided by your doctor. (*See* OEDEMA *and* MURMUR.)

Heartblock
A condition in which the electrical impulses, from atrium to ventricle, are blocked by disease in the 'conducting' tissue. Causes are as for heart disease. These impulses regulate the rate of heart beat and if blocked the heart beats too slowly for efficient circulation. Drugs may help but the insertion of an artificial pacemaker is necessary in most cases.

Heartburn
A form of indigestion in which burning pain is felt in the centre of the chest. It may be associated with hiatus hernia. (*See* HIATUS HERNIA.)

Hemiplegia
A condition in which one half of the body becomes paralysed. It is due to some disturbance of the brain, and most commonly follows a stroke. (*See* STROKE.)

Hepatitis

Inflammation of the liver. The liver may be attacked by viruses either from the blood stream or the digestive tract. When this happens the bile is sometimes unable to escape from the liver, and so passes back into the blood stream causing jaundice. (*See* JAUNDICE, ALCOHOLISM, GALL BLADDER *and* LIVER.) Hepatitis virus is endemic in Africa and Asia and travellers should be inoculated against it.

Herbal Remedies

The beneficial actions of certain herbs have long been known. Even today some of the most important remedies are derived from herbs, e.g. the heart drug digitalis which is obtained from the foxglove leaf. An interesting new finding is that onions and garlic reduce the levels of cholesterol in our blood and perhaps reduce heart disease. Whilst valuing 'natural' medicines we should not disparage new technology which has enabled us to benefit from synthetic medicines.

Hernia (*Rupture*) (*See* HIATUS HERNIA.)

The space within the abdomen is taken up by a number of organs, including the intestines which form a long coiled tube (*Fig. 1, page 35*). The walls of the abdomen, in front, are made of layers of muscle, and, if a weakness develops, one coil of intestine may push between the muscle layers and come to lie under the skin. It is known as a hernia. The common site is the groin, the weakest part of the abdomen, particularly in men where there is an opening through which the cord passes to the testis. If this becomes stretched a rupture may develop. Ruptures occur in other positions, around the navel or at the site of old operation scars. The best treatment is often an operation. If the space through which the intestine protrudes can be firmly sewn up, the rupture will be cured.

A hernia may be caused by lifting heavy weights or

chronic coughing, etc. Smokers must give up smoking before and after the operation.

Most hernias show as a painless swelling in the groin which gets larger on coughing, straining, etc. Pain occurs when the contents of a hernia become twisted or nipped. The hernia may then be painful and may not reduce back into the abdomen on lying down. Urgent surgical treatment is then required.

Herpes

A virus causing a group of spots on an area of inflamed skin. The spots (vesicles) have white heads containing fluid. There are two types. Herpes Zoster is the name for shingles (*see* SHINGLES); and another variety Herpes Simplex which develops in areas such as the lips – usually during other illness, e.g. a cold. Keep the spots dry. They can be dabbed with surgical spirit from time to time and dusted with talcum powder. They usually disappear in days leaving no marks. A variant of Herpes Simplex affects the genital area (*see* SEXUALLY TRANSMITTED DISEASES). Herpes can be treated in its early stages by applying Zovirax cream four times daily and if severe by Zovirax tablets.

Hiatus Hernia

An internal hernia where the upper part of the stomach bulges through the opening in the diaphragm intended for the passage of the gullet. The acid stomach contents can thus pass into the sensitive gullet causing pain and inflammation. The condition is aggravated by over-weight, and wearing tight corsets. Stooping for house-hold tasks and lying flat in bed cause the acid to flow into the gullet. Bending should be done at the knee joint only and the head of the bed raised on books or bricks. Antacids and medicines are helpful. The operation to cure is a large one and reserved for severe cases.

Hiccough

This can be distressing if it refuses to stop. It is usually due to an irritation of the stomach which causes a spasmodic contraction of the breathing muscles resulting in the familiar 'hic'. One or two glasses of water will often cut an attack short as will firm pinching of the nose for one minute. Recurrent attacks can indicate hiatus hernia (*see* HIATUS HERNIA) or other illness so medical investigation is necessary.

Hodgkin's Disease (*Lymphoma*)
A form of cancer of the lymph glands (*see* GLANDS). Advances in the last few years mean that this cancer is now readily curable. Symptoms include very enlarged rubbery glands in the neck, armpits or groins. Seek early advice.

Homosexuality
Sexual attraction towards those of the same sex (usually taken to mean males). Almost everyone is to some extent bi-sexual. If a homosexual is well-adjusted there is no medical indication for treatment. Claims are made that sometimes psychiatric treatment may reverse the condition.

It is normal for some young people to have some homosexual inclinations during their teens and perhaps even into the late twenties. This is a quite usual phase of sexual awakening and they should not make the mistake of thinking that they must be homosexual for life, or allow themselves to be led unnecessarily in this direction. Much active homosexuality is indulged in experimentally and for excitement rather than need.

Some authorities believe that the male homosexual population is a reservoir of VD infection. Steady partners are harder to find, so casual sex is more common although AIDS has caused more careful behaviour in most homosexuals. (*See* LESBIANISM.)

Hookworm
A worm found in dirty water in many parts of the

140

world. It causes stomach upsets and severe anaemia.

Hormones
Chemical substances secreted directly into the blood by ductless glands, they affect various body functions. The sex hormones are only one of many types. Where glands are diseased, replacement of the appropriate hormone can often be carried out artificially. This is the rationale for hormone replacement therapy during and after the menopause (*see* MENOPAUSE) when the ovary reduces its production of oestrogen.

Huntington's Chorea
A progressive disease of the nervous system which runs in families. Symptoms begin in early middle age and include jerky involuntary movements and intellectual impairment. The Association to Combat Huntington's Chorea provides information and help for families of sufferers.

Hydrocoele
A collection of fluid in the scrotum. It can be present at birth or may develop later in life. Not serious but it can be uncomfortable. Drawing the fluid off via a needle gives temporary relief but the best treatment is by a minor operation.

Hypertension
(*See* BLOOD PRESSURE.)

Hypnosis
Hypnosis is defined as a sleep-like state in which the phenomena of hallucination, memory disturbance and altered behaviour can be induced. However, this relates to the deep state which is less common and for practical purposes hypnosis in most subjects can be regarded as a state of mental and physical relaxation.

The lay concept of hypnosis is usually related to 'showbiz' with its dramatic presentation. But what hypnosis is and how it works remains a mystery. Hence methods of induction and clinical uses are still evolving. Traditionally it is used in varied conditions including asthma, migraine and colitis, in the neuroses, in childbirth and gynaecology and in skin diseases and dentistry.

But its most useful applications are in general practice and relate to the many stress reactions people produce to problems of work, finance, housing and marriage and to unpleasant experiences such as a burglary, thunderstorms and examinations, and to assist people to stop smoking and lose weight. Only simple probing of the patient's psyche and past history is necessary in most cases. Simple symptom removal or, preferably, symptom tolerance may well be the best useful method in the future. With increasing tolerance and acceptance, the psychological overlay or 'hang-up' that people get to problems diminishes and this may be followed by a reduction in the patient's stress reaction to their life style. Sometimes hypnosis does not help, other times only to a limited degree, for, like many treatments, it is not magic. But it is worth attempting especially if traditional remedies have failed, for if at worst nothing happens, then at best, the quality of life is enriched. Good results are not uncommon but no guarantee can ever be given.

Hypothermia

Abnormally low body temperature (*see* TEMPERATURE). Elderly people and babies are less able to maintain normal temperature and in cold weather require their homes to have more heat than the average. For such people a room temperature of 70°F or 21°C should be ideal – but people differ greatly in needs. Hypothermia often occurs when the elderly patient gets an illness such as a cold or 'flu and becomes house-bound and isolated – keep an eye on your elderly neighbours during the winter.

Hysterectomy
Operation to remove the womb. The womb is a wonderful container for the developing baby but has no effect on femininity in general. Since one or both ovaries are often retained after this operation the woman need not fear loss of femininity or sudden 'menopause' symptoms. If the ovaries must be removed before the menopause because of cysts or other disease, the patient is usually given hormone replacement tablets.

Hysterectomy is usually performed because of heavy, painful periods often due to fibroids. The relief of discarding the source of blood loss usually greatly outweighs the disadvantages of an operation. After six to twelve weeks the woman should feel fully recovered and sexual intercourse can usually be resumed after the first follow-up appointment.

Hysterectomy has no effect on vague ill-health, depression and menopause symptoms like flushing. Women should not imagine that hysterectomy is a cure for all the ills of middle age. It may precipitate or aggravate depression already present. Women suffering from such symptoms should seek advice from their doctor or counsellor.

Hysteria
A nervous disorder in which the sufferer develops impressive symptoms such as total paralysis, total loss of voice, total loss of sensation in the absence of any physical disease. The patient's previous personality has often shown a tendency to exaggerated mood swings. The illness brings some gain e.g. attention or a means of escape from an unpleasant situation but the mental process is not deliberate as in malingering. Hysteria also has a popular meaning when applied to a person

who loses control. Following some shock the patient may fling and squirm, go into uncontrollable laughter or tears. A firm hand and sharp words, rather than sympathy, usually produce good results.

I

Ichthyosis
A dry and scaly skin condition which sometimes runs in families. It can be alleviated by keeping the skin constantly greased with special ointments or baby oil.

Ileostomy
Artificial opening of the small intestine (ileum) on to the front abdominal wall. This operation is usually performed where most of the large bowel (colon) is diseased, as in ulcerative colitis, and needs to be removed. Unlike cancer, this condition often occurs in young people so there are many healthy young people around, coping well with this problem. Although the contents of the small bowel are liquid they are odourless so this particular embarrassment is avoided. Disposable polythene bags and attachments make this condition quite easy to manage and much preferable to the miseries of severe colitis. The Ileostomy Association of Great Britain and Ireland exists to give advice and support where necessary. (*See* COLOSTOMY.)

Immunisation (*Vaccination*)
Protection against disease by the introduction into a susceptible person of a killed or weakened germ in small quantities so as to induce the production of antibodies. Small, modified amounts of the poison normally produced by the germ may be used instead. The antibodies produced are effective against the real germ in spite of having been produced by weaker substances. Doses of vaccine may need to be given

more than once in order to achieve full immunity. Boosters are often necessary after a few years. (*See* WHOOPING COUGH, DIPHTHERIA, POLIOMYELITIS, TETANUS, MEASLES, GERMAN MEASLES *and* MUMPS.)

Impetigo

An infectious skin disease caused by a germ – the streptococcus. It usually attacks the face and scalp and is common in children. A small area of skin becomes itchy and inflamed – often near the corner of the mouth – and then begins to weep and form yellowish crusts. If not treated it tends to spread rapidly. Because of this, suspected cases of impetigo are best taken to a doctor as early as possible. It responds to antibiotics (such as penicillin) which are best given by mouth. The area affected must be kept dry, and efforts made to prevent the patient scratching, for this is one of the chief factors spreading the infection. Bed linen, pillows, handkerchieves and washing materials should be kept strictly separate, and they should be well boiled before being returned to general use.

Impotence

Inability to perform intercourse by the male. The cause is either bodily or in the mind. Among the usually curable *physical* reasons are: a 'stone' pressing on the urethra, interference with the nervous system due to accident or illness such as diabetes. Excessive alcohol or a broken heart can shut down virility until the cause is removed. Prolonged love-making can exhaust the system temporarily. Hormone imbalance may occasionally be the cause. One of the commonest causes nowadays is treatment with modern drugs for high blood pressure or heart problems.

However, allowing that physical causes can co-exist with psychological, causes in the mind may be responsible for over ninety-five per cent of impotence, in the sense that when the worries disappear, cure follows.

146

Often the bodily cause arrives after the psychological one, because body and mind affect each other. Proof is that as soon as the impotent man's confidence is restored, so is his virility.

Sex fears and taboos go back thousands of years, and some still lurk in the backwaters of our minds. In Victorian times this was perhaps understandable, but since then many pioneering books on sex have been published. Today the enquirer is likely rather to be perplexed by the wide variety of advice available in cheap paperback form. These books reflect the views and prejudices of their authors. Here, however, are a few truths:

Masturbation normally does no harm. Almost every human being has done it, and it is a necessary outlet for those with no partner.

Failure to obtain erection is mainly caused by *fear of failure*, depression or other anxieties. With repeated failure, this fear can feed upon itself. The cure is success, and faith!

Successful erection results when the penis fills with blood due to friction, mental stimulation, or preferably both. Arousal follows kissing, love play, fantasising, or maybe after reading a passionate novel, etc.

Premature ejaculation is a common associated problem. It may even happen before intercourse has started. It is usually caused by a (quite natural) urge to hurry to 'get in' before ejaculation. Slow it down and play it cool! If you feel your orgasm coming during foreplay, stop and rest. Pause and breathe deeply which strengthens control. Finally, enter the vagina at a snail's pace, stopping for a while if you feel orgasm coming too early. A second attempt should be more successful; the point is you cannot damage yourself for Nature does not allow that. If you try too often, the penis refuses to rise until rested, that's all.

Be reassured that (provided there is no extraordinary physical cause) nobody can begin a week virile and end it impotent. Sex problems are not a sign of cowardice. Do not feel guilty. Impotence is not an illness but a symptom and almost always curable.

Love-plays can be an occasional alternative to intercourse and sometimes temporarily the only enjoyment following accidents or for the handicapped who have sex needs too. (*See* FRIGIDITY, HOMOSEXUALITY, PROSTATE.)

Incontinence
This is when control over the bladder or the bowel is lost. By the age of three bladder control should be established (*see* ENURESIS). The bladder exit is guarded by a muscle; normally it is when we allow this muscle to relax that urine is passed. Incontinence results from many causes. In both sexes it will occur when the nervous control of the bladder is disturbed. Thus a patient may become incontinent after a STROKE when part of the brain is damaged, or an injury to the spine in a road accident. Diseases of the bladder or neighbouring parts may also cause incontinence. Thus it may occur temporarily in CYSTITIS or in prolapse. (*See* PROLAPSE.) Loss of bowel control is also usually due to spinal damage or STROKE. Occasionally in the elderly it is associated with extreme constipation when 'spurious' diarrhoea results. Whatever the cause it calls for expert treatment; and anyone who finds difficulty in controlling these functions should consult a doctor. (*See* PARALYSIS, PROSTATE.)

Indigestion
This term covers a host of symptoms, and is used when there is any upset in normal digestion. It may be applied to discomfort or pain following meals, heartburn or flatulence. In a medical sense the term has no precise meaning, and does not refer to any definite disease. (*See* ACIDOSIS, DUODENAL ULCER, DYSPEPSIA, FLATULENCE *and* GASTRIC ULCER.)

Infant Feeding (*and Failure to Thrive*)

In general, breast milk (which comes in sterile containers at the right temperature!) is best for feeding babies, certainly for the first six to nine months. A few mothers will be unable to do this and can be reassured that carefully prepared bottle feeds provide a good alternative. However, it now seems certain that many mothers who in the past felt obliged to give up breast feeding for reasons like 'insufficient milk', engorgement, etc., were probably just lacking the right advice and management at the crucial early stages. In some surveys breast-fed babies have been found to have fewer infections, weight problems or allergies and less coeliac disease, and in later life less heart disease, and less dental decay. Your health visitor will also be able to advise you before and after the baby arrives.

One of the secrets of success is total demand feeding without bottle supplements from the earliest hours. This may mean as many as ten feeds a day for the first month reducing in succeeding months. Milk supply depends on frequent sucking, not on some 'inherent' factor in the breast. Engorgement is usually due to too infrequent feeds or a rigid schedule. You should feed your baby when he cries, if your breasts feel full, whenever 'you feel like it' and if he goes for as long as four hours without a feed. It is possible to underfeed a young baby who may sleep for long periods giving the illusion of contentment. Sadly, this can lead to an apparently 'contented' baby being severely undernourished. *Few babies under three months can manage on less than five daily feeds*.

The bottle-fed baby has a minor advantage as his feeds can be measured. As a rough guide a young baby needs 2½ oz milk per pound of body weight daily. Thus after the first week, a seven pound baby needs 17½ oz milk divided into five or six feeds i.e. approximately 3 oz at a time. Baby will take different amounts at different times but this gives some idea.

Babies gain roughly 4 to 7 oz of weight weekly in the early months. If they *consistently* fail to do so it usually means something is wrong and advice from the health visitor or doctor is needed. Apart from the usual cause, which is a feeding problem, the others are infection, particularly in the waterworks and, rarely, congenital defects such as heart disease.

Solid food such as cereal should not be offered until six weeks at the earliest, but many small babies cannot cope with any solid food until two or three months. A proprietary brand of rice suitable for infants is one of the least stodgy solids to begin with. One teaspoon with one of the daily feeds is enough to start and you can gradually build up over the subsequent months. Sieved vegetables and fruit and finally meat meals can be introduced slowly. Baby will probably have fads and fancies but do not worry about it as milk supplemented by vitamin drops is his most important food for the first nine or ten months. When teething begins, around six months, he will, of course, want to bite on something a little harder such as a rusk; but he is unlikely to eat more than half of it. The nutritional value of a rusk is similar to cereal.

A relaxed mother is likely to have less problems with feeds than a mother who is tense, so she should aim to put aside a little time daily for her own interests and relaxation.

Infantile Paralysis
(*See* POLIOMYELITIS.)

Infection
This occurs when the body is invaded by germs. It may be local as in a boil, or a generalised infection like measles. A disease is *infectious* when the germs can be spread indirectly from person to person. Thus 'colds' are infectious, being spread by coughing and sneezing. Some diseases are spread by direct contact and these

are *contagious*. An example is venereal disease in which the germs are normally spread only by sexual contact with a diseased person.

Infertility

Properly thought of as sub-fertility for few people are totally infertile. Pregnancy occurs when an egg (released monthly from the woman's ovaries) passes into the Fallopian tube and is fertilised by a male sperm. This fertilised egg continues along the tube to the womb where it embeds in the soft lining. This process requires that all is well with the overies, tubes, uterus lining, cervix and vagina. The ovary is influenced by the pituitary gland below the brain and is subject to nervous factors.

In the man the mechanism of erection and ejaculation must operate, the production of sperms by the testicle must be satisfactory in quality and quantity and there must be an unblocked passage along the male tube (vas) along to the storage pouch (seminal vesicle) and then on into the passage through the penis. Fluid from the prostate gland is also added to the semen at ejaculation. Most couples are probably infertile at some time after a bout of influenza or a period of exhaustion.

The ovum is usually released about day 14 of the average twenty-eight day period cycle (counting the first day of a period as day one). Both egg and sperm have a limited life – not more than one to two days – so only intercourse on day 13 to 16 approximately is liable to result in pregnancy (this cannot be relied on for contraception – *see* CONTRACEPTION).

If after six months to a year of being in good health and having had intercourse at least three times a week, especially at mid-cycle, there is still no sign of a baby, it is worth seeing a doctor to see if there is some easily remedied cause. One assumes that this healthy young couple are taking a balanced diet, plenty of protein, fibre foods and vitamins, also exercise and joy in each other's company.

Sometimes the reassurance of the feeling that 'something is being done' provides the necessary relaxation and it is common to find the woman is pregnant by the time her specialist appointment comes along!

While waiting for a gynaecological appointment a woman can obtain a good idea of whether or not she is ovulating (releasing an egg) regularly by recording her oral, early morning temperature before rising or having any drink. This should be charted against date and the day of her period cycle. A tiny fall followed immediately by a half degree F (¼°C) rise which continues until the end of the cycle indicates ovulation. If this is occurring regularly there is no problem with ovulation.

Sometimes minor abnormalities such as small fibroids, an erosion (ulcer on the neck of the womb) or backward tilting of the womb are found and these can often be corrected surgically with good results. Blocked tubes due either to advanced appendicitis, tuberculosis or venereal disease are a more difficult problem. The promiscuous nineteen-year-old rarely spares a thought for her future sorry state at 30+ with blocked tubes and the adoption waiting lists closed. Operations to unblock them are not over-successful, although Fallopian tube transplants are being tried. Sometimes where tubes are blocked by threadlike adhesions they can be cleared by insufflation with carbon dioxide.

Test Tube Baby
The test tube baby technique as used in the UK was devised to overcome a problem of totally blocked tubes due to appendicitis. A method was devised for estimating exactly the time of ovulation and an egg was removed from the ovary at this point. The minor operation done under a general anaesthetic was performed through a type of telescope (the laparoscope) so that a minute incision only was necessary. The egg

was mixed with the husband's fresh semen in a tube and was re-implanted into the womb lining at night (apparently the best time for a 'take'). Thereafter pregnancy continued in the normal way. This is the most *extreme* form of AIH (Artificial Insemination Husband).

In less extreme cases the gynaecologist can place the husband's semen directly in the neck of the womb, via a syringe, where there is some problem like unusual position of cervix, a potency problem, etc. Where there is a low sperm count, several specimens of the husband's semen can be centrifuged and a more concentrated liquid inserted.

To consider the male aspect a little more. A simple semen test arranged by the family doctor may show anything from a satisfactory vigorous number of sperms to fewer sperms or some condition needing treatment. Sometimes even the healthy ones become sluggish on contact with the mucus contained in the woman's cervix. This can be confirmed by a test on the woman some hours after intercourse. Even complete absence of sperm in the seminal fluid may simply mean a blockage somewhere along the sperm-collecting tubes whilst sperm production by the testicle is normal; this may be amenable to plastic surgery. Sometimes the position corrects itself.

If nothing further can be done to help the man's problem whereas his wife has normal fertility the question of AID (Artificial Insemination Donor) arises. Often the couple wish to have a child that is at least part their own flesh and blood and if both parties are in agreement the technique is similar to that of AIH. The voluntary donor is always young and healthy, often a medical student. Total secrecy is maintained as to his identity.

Here are some small tips which may help a couple who do not so far feel that medical help is necessary. Since in intercourse the semen has to travel along the cervical canal, through the uterus and up the Fallopian tube, it may help if the woman remains on her back with her hips raised on a pillow for twenty minutes after intercourse; even better if the couple remain in this position together, without moving much.

If the uterus is tilted backwards the sperms tend to be deposited behind the cervix rather than onto it. Intercourse in which the man enters from behind helps to place the semen in the right place. It is worth trying this position several times even if you are not sure in which position your womb is lying.

Abstention from intercourse for a few days increases the sperm count but this should not be taken to extremes. A three day abstension before intercourse at estimated ovulation time is all that is necessary.

Often after many tests the specialists tell you that they cannot find any reason why you should not conceive. Although in these circumstances a baby may arrive seven to ten years or more after your anxieties first began, it is possibly wise to approach the adoption agencies. Although white, healthy babies under a year are in short supply there are babies of mixed race, and some with handicaps, and some older children available.

Inflammation
The reaction of a body tissue to injury – provided the injury is not sufficient to kill the part. It does not matter much what form the injury takes: traumas, heat, cold or infection. The part becomes swollen and red because the small blood vessels are widely opened; for the same reason it is usually painful because nerve endings are irritated. An example is a boil which shows the characteristic signs of inflammation, being swollen, red, hot, and painful.

Influenza
An acute generalised infection which occurs in epidemics. Several different types of virus cause slightly

different kinds of 'flu. The disease usually starts with a fever and aches and pains in limbs, back and head. The patient feels unwell and alternately hot and shivery. There may be watering of eyes and nose followed by a sore throat and irritating cough. Later on, sickness may be a feature and in this case the illness is often spoken of as 'gastric flu'. It is not usually serious, though there have been severe epidemics. The temperature settles down usually within a week, and the patient gradually returns to health. It is chiefly dangerous because it lowers the body's defences and may be followed by complications like pneumonia. It is not a condition to neglect, and the patient should remain in bed until the temperature is normal for 24 hours. Depression is common following influenza and convalescence should not be hurried.

There is at present no specific treatment for influenza. Antibiotics are not a cure; they are only of use for complications like bronchitis. Vaccines have been developed for many strains of influenza; if given in October they can be effective for the winter. Alas, the influenza virus frequently changes and becomes resistant to the vaccines. Protection against one epidemic will not necessarily protect against the next.

Ingrowing Toe Nail
This is common. The surrounding skin fold becomes raised at the edge so that the nail instead of growing over grows *into* it causing pain. The skin fold often becomes infected and may discharge pus. It may be due to tight shoes, particularly in childhood. To prevent it, care should be given to fitting shoes especially in the young (*see also* BURSA). The nails should be cut straight across, *not into an oval*, and the services of a chiropodist are often worthwhile. For severe cases it is sometimes necessary to have a small operation and antibiotics may be required to treat the infection.

Insanity
(*See* MENTAL ILLNESS.)

Insomnia
Inability to sleep is a tiring condition. It becomes common with age. Those troubled should read the section on Sleep, page 13. If that does not cure, consult a doctor. Often simple remedies such as covering the eyes over to keep out the light or, if noise prevents sleep, several types of earplugs may be helpful. A hot bottle to cold feet can do the trick. Thinking happy thoughts, a sexless cuddle of one's mate or intercourse can work, but possibly a holiday, away from it all, is best. Some people find sitting up supported by pillows or using an extra pillow helps, unless they happen to have any neck trouble. A well-made bed is important; if the sheet is not wrapped to cover the blankets, the latter can tickle the face and prevent sleep.

Insulin
A hormone produced by the pancreas which controls the rate the body burns up sugar and starchy food. (*See* DIABETES, GLANDS, HORMONES.)

Intussusception
Where one part of the intestine telescopes into another. Sufferers are usually male babies between six and twelve months old who suffer severe colic, accompanied by screaming and drawing up of the knees. Often there is sickness, and in some a little dark red blood is passed from the bowels. The condition calls for urgent treatment to correct the problem as an operation is required.

Iritis
A serious but readily treated cause of a red painful eye. It is due to inflammation of the iris (coloured part of the eye which acts as a diaphragm to light). The pupil is

156

usually small and the iris seems cloudly in this condition. Urgent treatment is required. (*See* EYES.)

Irritable Bowel Syndrome

This condition, more common in women, consists of abdominal discomfort and alteration of bowel habits. No physical cause can be found. Various treatments are available to help symptoms; most important is reassurance that there is no disease.

Itch (*See also* SCABIES.)

Caused by mild irritation of the skin, it is a common symptom of many skin diseases. Scratching cures an itch temporarily by swamping the messages which travel up the nerves by more powerful ones; but in the long run it often makes it worse by increasing the irritation. For a mild itchiness calamine lotion is often effective. If it is not, see your doctor as there is possibly a skin condition which can be treated.

J

Jaundice

One function of the liver (*see* LIVER) is to make bile, a dark green liquid stored beneath the liver in a pouch known as the GALL BLADDER. It pours into the intestine where it helps the digestion of fats. If the bile cannot escape into the bowel it is forced back into the liver and enters the blood stream. The skin and the whites of the eyes then become coloured yellow (the former not visible in the yellow or coloured races). This is *jaundice*. Whatever the cause the sufferer usually feels *extremely* ill with vomiting, no appetite and abdominal pain. There are many causes.

(1) Jaundice can occur in new-born infants due to the immaturity of the liver which cannot quite cope with its various functions. This type usually clears within days but can be treated by ultraviolet ray therapy if necessary. Where there is incompatability between the parents' blood groups, especially of the rhesus factor (*see* RHESUS FACTOR), the jaundice may be more serious. If ultraviolet ray treatment is not effective, exchange blood transfusions may be needed.

(2) Infectious hepatitis (*see* HEPATITIS) – the liver may be attacked by viruses which cause inflammation, damaging liver cells and blocking the ducts which carry the bile. Other germs and viruses can also attack the liver. Sometimes GLANDULAR FEVER is complicated by jaundice.

(3) Mechanical blockage of the bile ducts always leads to jaundice. Sometimes stones develop in the gall

bladder and one of these may obstruct the duct which takes bile into the intestine. This duct may also be blocked by enlarged lymph glands or by a tumour.

(4) Excessive destruction of red blood cells which occurs in some types of anaemia can lead to jaundice.

(5) Damage to liver cells by poisons can cause jaundice. Such poisons include carbon tetrachloride used in dry cleaning, some of the poisonous toadstools and excessive consumption of alcohol. (*See* ALCOHOLISM.)

All types of jaudice need urgent medical attention. In young people the commonest form is infectious hepatitis. It is spread by infected food and drink and sometimes by direct person-to-person contact. A similar but much more serious form of hepatitis, known as serum hepatitis is acquired directly from infected blood and can be transmitted by dirty syringes and occasionally by blood transfusion (rarely in the UK). This is why a person with a past history of jaundice can never be a blood donor. It is possible to be a carrier of the disease for many years while feeling perfectly well. Drug addicts dependent on shots of heroin from dirty syringes risk serum hepatitis and the disease can be transmitted by sexual intercourse among casual contacts who may be carriers, commonly found among homosexuals.

Treatment of infectious hepatitis consists of bed rest, low fat diet and complete abstinence from alcohol. Alcohol should not be taken for at least six months, even though the symptoms may have cleared in the first weeks. Relapse of jaundice can occur if this rule is not obeyed. Cases of serum hepatitis may need to be admitted to specialist hospital units for intensive treatment.

Jugular Vein
A large vein in the neck, draining blood from the brain and skull to the heart.

K

Kidney Diseases

The kidneys are two organs at the back of the abdominal cavity. They filter the blood continually passing through them, and remove waste products which are then disposed of in the urine. The kidneys may be the seat of acute inflammation known as *nephritis*. Symptoms are pain in the loins, fever and the dark red urine due to the presence of blood. There may also be swelling beneath the eyes and the lower parts of the body due to water in the tissues (*see* OEDEMA). Urgent medical treatment is needed.

Sometimes infection ascends the kidney tubes from the bladder leading to pyelonephritis. In this there is usually a high temperature, pain in the loins, and great frequency in passing water. This infection needs urgent investigation and treatment with antibiotics.

In some patients severe disease may result in failure of the kidney to remove poisonous waste products from the blood. (*See* URAEMIA.) Modern treatments have revolutionised the outlook for these people. Artificial kidney machines often installed in the patient's own home can replace the work of the patient's own kidneys by filtering the blood. Sufferers are usually 'plugged in' three nights a week and they and their families become adept at handling the apparently complicated machinery. Many are helped by kidney transplants when a suitable 'matching' donor kidney is available. Transplant patients need continual treatment with drugs to prevent their rejecting the new kidney, but they usually feel remarkably well.

We can all help such patients by agreeing to make our kidneys available for transplant after our death. Kidney donor cards for signature by donor and next-of-kin are available in doctor's surgeries, hospital out-patients departments and Local Authority Clinics.

Sometimes stones develop in the kidney and escape, causing pain and bleeding as they pass down the duct (or ureter) from the kidney to the bladder. Medical investigation is necessary. (*See* CALCULUS *and* RENAL COLIC.)

Knock-Knee

A condition in which the ankles are some distance apart when the knees are placed together. This is commonly seen in healthy young children and will correct sponta-neously in ninety-nine per cent of cases. Provided that the distance between the ankles is not greater than 10cm (4 ins) in a four-year-old the parents can be reassured that the condition should be corrected without treatment. In the few persistent cases, ortho-paedic stapling or operation near maturity when the bones are matured give good results.

Bow legs (which curve outwards below the knee, and then back in again) in British children are rarely due to dietary deficiency and again are normal in many toddlers who grow out of the condition by the age of four. Rickets due to inadequate vitamin D may be a cause in Asian and other children. Treatment here is by extra vitamin D (cod liver oil), calcium (syrup of calcium gluconate) and orthopaedic manoeuvres. In later life, bone disease such as Pagets can cause bowing of the legs.

Kwashiorkor

A deficiency disease in small children occurring in areas of the world where chronic malnutrition occurs. It is mainly due to protein deficiency and results in the child being prone to dysentery and other infections. Typically the child is pot-bellied, apathetic and miserable. Treatment is correction of all the deficiencies and the infections present.

L

Labia
Derived from Latin; it means lips. It is the name for the double folds of skin which form part of the external female organs. There are two labia, an inner and outer on each side of the mid-line. Close to the inner pair are a number of small glands (*see* BARTHOLIN'S GLANDS) whose function is to lubricate the part during sexual intercourse.

Labour
(*See* BIRTH.)

Laryngitis
The larynx (voice box) lies in the neck at the top of the windpipe, below the throat. It is liable to become inflamed in any infection of the respiratory (breathing) organs, and laryngitis may follow or accompany such conditions as a 'cold' or bronchitis. It often starts with 'tickling' low in the throat followed by a cough, which becomes painful. If the attack is severe, the larynx cannot function properly so that the voice becomes husky, sometimes only a whisper. The condition usually clears in about a week, provided that voice rest is carried out. It can be relieved by inhaling steam to which soothing medicaments such as Friars' Balsam (one teaspoon to a pint) have been added. Honey and lemon preparations are soothing but if the condition is not improving consult your doctor.

Legionnaires' Disease

This is a bacterial infection which tends to occur in outbreaks due to the bacteria being present in faulty air conditioning systems or cooling towers. It has not been shown to spread from person to person. It may be mild or a severe illness affecting the lungs, abdomen or nervous system, and often presents as a chest infection in the form of acute pneumonia. Fortunately it responds to antibiotics such as erythromycin. Hospital admission is necessary in the elderly and in severe cases.

Leishmaniasis (Kala-azar)

A tropical disease in which a microscopic protozoa causes chronic fever and anaemia. It is spread by sand-flies and presents with chronic skin ulcers and is characterised by gross enlargement of the spleen.

Leprosy

A chronic disease once found all over the world but now only seen in India, Africa, Asia and the Pacific. It is caused by the leprosy bacillus (Hansen's) and leads to loss of pigment in the skin, skin ulceration and thickening of the nerves causing loss of sensation. As a result, tissue destruction and increasing deformity take place over a period of years.

It can now be treated with antibiotics and, because it is now realised that it is not very infectious, is no longer the dread disease which led to the 'lepers' being rejected by society.

Leptospirosis (Weil's Disease)

An infection transmitted in water from infected rats (and occasionally dogs). It is found all over the world and causes fever, jaundice and kidney failure. If treated early with antibiotics it usually responds.

Lesbianism (*See also* HOMOSEXUALITY.)

Sexual attraction between two women.

Leucorrhoea

The name given to slight excess of the *normal* creamy white discharge from the vagina. There is normally more discharge at puberty, when the sexual functions are becoming established, also for a few days before each period, and often during pregnancy. This type of discharge is never irritant or offensive. Any discharge which seems more than normal leucorrhoea, is offensive, or which causes soreness, itching or irritation must be investigated. Your doctor is used to such matters and it is better to have the condition put right early. (*See* GONORRHOEA, NSU, VAGINITIS.)

Leukaemia

The name given to a disease in which the white cells or corpuscles in the blood multiply. The function of white cells is chiefly to deal with invading germs, and their number is normally relatively low compared to red cells. The condition of *leukaemia* may be regarded as a form of cancer in which the white cells continue to multiply indiscriminately. There are many types of leukaemia. The white cells can be broadly divided into two categories known as lymphocytes and myelocytes.

Acute leukaemia of the lymphocytes occurs in young children and is thus one of the most distressing forms of cancer. Modern methods of treatment are however giving promising results. Treatment with special drugs and radiation can keep the disease suppressed in ninety per cent of children, and patients treated with marrow transplantation are usually permanently cured. These treatments are complicated and must be given in specialist centres. Symptoms at the onset are vague but include persistent tiredness and listlessness. Usually there is a simple explanation like the common childhood infections or mild anaemia but if the parents are worried a simple blood test will establish the facts.

Similar types of treatment for the types of *acute* leukaemia which occur in young adults are showing similar results to those obtained in children. In older people the *chronic* leukaemias can be treated with drugs only, obtaining good results in most cases. Such patients can often lead normal lives for years after the original diagnosis.

Lice

Small animal parasites, the size of a match head. They live on the human body and usually inhabit hairy regions, cementing their eggs, or nits, to a hair after they are laid. There are three families: the head louse, the body louse, and the pubic louse. *Pediculosis* is the medical term for infestation by lice. The condition is contagious as lice spread from one person to another. Infection by body lice is encouraged by lack of personal cleanliness. Lice flourish when washing becomes difficult, as for instance, in fighting soldiers. The louse feeds on blood from its host, and the bites cause irritation. Scratching may introduce germs so that infected spots and small boils develop. A grave consequence is the spreading of a disease known as TYPHUS, a serious illness caused by a small germ which, apart from attacking a man, can live in the body of the louse. Infected lice may spread from person to person, carrying the disease with them.

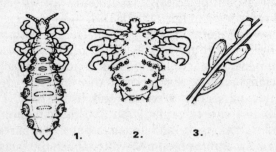

Fig. 9 Lice

1 Body louse   **2** Pubic louse   **3** Nit

166

Pubic lice are commonly transmitted by sexual activity and other tests for venereal disease should always be carried out where pubic 'crabs' are found.

Unlike the body lice, *head* lice are no respectors of personal cleanliness and will spread rapidly round a clean room of clean school children if one child has them.

Treatment of head and pubic lice is usually by malathion liquid left on for thirty minutes, then shampooed off. Body lice can be treated by quellada lotion applied to the whole body except the head and left on for 24 hours before washing off. The hair is combed with a fine-tooth comb before drying to remove nits. Treatment can be repeated in 48 hours.

Limp

In general, a limp is nature's way of protecting an injured limb from undue strain and of indicating a disorder. An injury to a limb is bound to produce some degree of limp for a time.

However, a limp occurring without a preceding injury in a child or teenager, between the ages of five and eighteen years, should never be ignored as there are two important medical problems which may be present and which should be caught in the early stages. Associated pain may be in the thigh, groin or even the knee. In one condition, the growing part of the top of the thigh bone slips out of place (*slipped epiphysis*) and if not corrected leads to a permanent limp and later arthritis. In the other disorder, the top of the thigh bone tends to become flattened and again the later development of arthritis is likely if the condition is neglected.

Babies at the crawling stage or who have just begun to walk need early medical attention if they consistently refuse to bear any weight or use an arm or leg. Whilst older children may occasionally limp in order to get attention, a limp in a toddler always means damage, possibly a fracture. Some babies are born with dislocated hips and although routine examination in the first weeks of life usually spots these; the occasional case is not diagnosed until walking is attempted. Treatment is by plaster or splinting and results are good. A limp or discrepancy in thigh length in newly walking babies therefore demands investigation.

Lipoma
The name given to a fatty tumour. The body is normally covered by a layer of fat beneath the skin, and sometimes, instead of being distributed evenly, the fat in one place forms into a soft, painless lump – about the size of an egg, beneath the skin. The tumours are harmless, but sometimes unsightly. They can easily be removed by operation.

Liver
A large organ in the upper right side of the abdominal cavity (*Fig. 1, page 35*); it serves important functions. The blood from the digestive tract passes through the liver before it returns to general circulation. A lot of the nourishment from food is altered by the liver to make it suitable for body use. Some food, particularly sugar, is stored in the liver so that it can be used later if the body requires it. The liver also removes worn-out blood corpuscles from the circulation and uses the red pigment (haemoglobin) from the red blood cells in the manufacture of the bile. This bile is stored in the GALL BLADDER and then poured into the intestine where it helps the digestion of fats. Inflammation of the liver is known as hepatitis (*see* HEPATITIS *and* JAUNDICE), and sometimes the cells degenerate so that the liver becomes scarred and can no longer carry out its functions properly; a condition known as *cirrhosis of the liver*. Although there are other causes, excessive alcohol is the most important cause of cirrhosis. You do not have to be an alcoholic to get cirrhosis; regular

social drinking of more than three pints of beer daily can cause damage. Unfortunately, women are more susceptible to cirrhosis than men and should limit their intake to two pints of beer daily. (*See* ALCOHOLISM.)

Loa-loa (*See also* FILARIASIS.)
An African tropical disease caused by a filaria worm and resulting in swellings of the skin called calabars. It is transmitted by flies.

Lobar Pneumonia
(*See* PNEUMONIA.)

Lumbago
(*See* BACKACHE.)

Lupus Vulgaris
A rare form of skin tuberculosis occasionally seen in tropical areas, readily treated with modern anti-tuberculous drugs.

Lymphadenoma or Lymphoma
(*See* HODGKIN'S DISEASE.)

M

Madura Foot

A chronic fungal infection affecting the feet and caused by a fungus called actinomyces found in rotting vegetation or wood.

Malaria

One of the commonest illnesses in the world, it is spread by the Anopheles mosquito. The tiny parasite is transferred by a bite to human red blood cells. Once established in the human blood it causes high fever, and prostrating illness which tends to recur. The Department of Health, of London, can advise you if your destination requires malaria protection. Anyone travelling to sub-tropical or tropical areas should take precautionary tablets such as Chloroquine 400 mgms weekly starting before they travel and for six weeks after returning.

Unfortunately, in many parts of the world Chloroquine resistance has occurred and it may be necessary to take an extra drug such as Nivaquin and Paludrine. Even so some patients will still develop malaria on return to the UK up to six weeks after infection. For this reason, anyone who has a fever within six weeks of return should always consult a doctor.

However in the Tropics precautions should be taken to avoid being bitten by using insect repellant sprays, bed mosquito netting, and clothing covering the body.

Mania and Hypomania (*See also* MENTAL ILLNESS.)

Terms covering abnormal states of excitement which

affect people who are subject to mood swings and it may be difficult to decide if there is illness or merely great energy. Mild cases (hypomania) appear restless, talkative and over-excited or may seem euphoric. Like all mental illnesses, mania can follow periods of prolonged stress. Manics can plunge into depression (*see* DEPRESSION) but the outlook is usually very good with prompt treatment.

It may be difficult for the patient with early hypomania to be persuaded to accept help as the euphoria leads him to believe he is healthy. Where there is a past history, one must watch for danger signs as the patient rarely complains. Advanced symptoms include euphoric ideas, etc., and sufferers become increasingly active driving themselves to exhaustion. The immediate essential is to control the exhausting, useless activity which can become frightening. A doctor will decide whether hospital treatment is indicated but if there is fear that the patient might harm himself or others in the interim, police aid must also be summoned.

During and after the acute stage, the patient should respond to medical treatment and later to psychological explanations including common sense discussion of the factors which have upset him. Such patients may need to take certain drugs such as Lithium as a preventive.

Mastitis
Inflammation of the breast which can lead to abscesses (*see* BREAST). The term is now often used to mean the discomfort which some women experience in the breast each month shortly before the period. It is due to fluid retention in the breasts and increase in glandular tissue which can be felt as general 'lumpiness' (not a single lump which requires urgent investigation). The monthly variation in female hormones accounts for these changes and some women seem more prone to this than others. If you are doubtful about nodules in

171

the breast do check with your doctor. They may well be due to this harmless condition but medical assessment is necessary. (*See* PREMENSTRUAL TENSION.)

Mastoid
The mastoid process is a projection from the bones of the skull behind the ear (*Fig. 6, page 102*). In common with several skull bones it is hollow (*see* ANTRUM), and contains small spaces filled with air. These spaces communicate with the inside of the ear, so if there is an untreated infection of the middle ear the mastoid may become involved. The condition, now rare, is known as *mastoiditis*. Prompt treatment of earache and ear infections with antibiotics has almost eliminated this condition.

Masturbation
Self-gratification of the sex urge. Among the young of both sexes it is common, normally harmless and preferable to promiscuity with its risks of illegitimate pregnancy, broken hearts or venereal disease.

Abnormal sperms are common after abstinence so regular release seems to have some beneficial effect on fertility. (*See* FRIGIDITY *and* IMPOTENCE.)

ME
(*See* POST-VIRAL FATIGUE SYNDROME.)

Measles
An infectious disease of childhood caused by a virus. The disease usually occurs in epidemics and commonly affects children, though older people who have escaped may develop it. A second attack is rare. The incubation period, i.e. the interval between 'catching' the germ and developing the disease, is usually about ten days. The early symptoms resemble a severe 'cold' and usually come on suddenly with shivering, headache, running and redness at the eyes and nose. A trouble-

some barking cough is a marked feature and the child is often brought to the doctor for 'chestiness'. The temperature rises gradually until the rash develops. This is usually on the fourth day, though before the spots develop on the skin they can be seen, often on the inside of the cheeks, as small red spots with a bluish-white centre.

The rash proper starts as small, dusky red slightly raised spots which soon run together, giving the skin a blotchy appearance. The spots appear behind the ears, then on the face, and later spread over the body. After about three days the rash usually begins to fade, the temperature settles, and the patient begins to recover. Measles is in fact an acute bronchitis with rash thrown in and mother will find she is looking after a very chesty child for a few days. Linctuses may be helpful and doctors may recommend antibiotics at the start of an attack to prevent complications.

The child needs rest and quiet, plenty of fluids and Paracetamol if he is achey or feverish. Since the disease lowers resistance, it may be followed by complications such as inflammation of the ears, and occasionally pneumonia. The patient may be given a full diet once the appetite returns.

Children are now offered inoculation against measles in their second year of life so this distressing disease should not occur. Parents fearing any brain damage from the vaccine should remember that brain inflammation is more likely from the disease itself.

Melaena
When blood escapes into the upper part of the digestive tract it becomes altered by the digestive juices, and is changed from red into a black, tarry semi-solid mass. The passage of this altered blood from the bowels is known as *melaena*. There are a number of causes. Bleeding from a gastric or duodenal ulcer may cause blood to pass into the intestines instead of being

173

brought up (*see* HAEMATEMESIS). Other diseases of the stomach and small bowel may also result in bleeding and melaena. Melaena is an indication of serious illness and prompt medical advice is needed.

Melanoma (*Mole*)
A benign tumour of the skin which may be brown or black due to the pigment melanin. Malignant change may occur in moles when the pigment cells multiply and become malignant (cancerous). This type of cancer is commoner in fair-skinned people over-exposed to sunlight. If a mole or freckle becomes larger, bleeds, itches or becomes sore, consult your doctor since this type of skin tumour is curable by a simple operation if caught early.

Meningitis
The meninges are layers of membrane which provide covering for the nervous tissue in the brain and spine. *Meningitis* is an inflammation of the meninges and *always needs urgent medical attention*. It may be caused by germs which attack the nervous system, and one in particular, the meningococcus can be responsible for epidemics. The onset in this type is sudden, and the most prominent symptom is very serious headache with stiffness of the neck. There is always fever, prostration and sometimes vomiting. In babies under a year its presentation is less obvious, the only symptoms being the vomiting of feeds, or unexplained fever. In babies the usual findings will be neck stiffness, irritability and if under 6 months a raised fontanelle. This form of meningitis responds to antibiotics if diagnosed and treated early.

Another form of meningitis, now rare in the UK, is caused by infection with the tubercle bacillus. The discovery of 'Streptomycin' and other antibiotics effective against the tubercle bacillus has greatly improved the outlook. The most common form of meningitis today is viral or aseptic meningitis. Symptoms are similar to meningococcal meningitis but the disease runs a milder course. Lumbar puncture and examination of the spinal fluid confirm the diagnosis. Treatment is usually by rest and analgesics. Nowadays complete recovery from viral meningitis is usual.

Menopause
Between 45 and 53 a woman normally becomes incapable of childbearing. Sometimes the periods stop suddenly, but in some women they become scanty or irregular before they finally cease. Many important bodily functions are controlled by various glands (including the ovaries) which pour hormones into the blood stream. These glands are under control of a 'master' gland, the pituitary, connected with the brain. At the menopause the ovaries gradually cease to function, and this often upsets the balance between the pituitary and other glands, so that it takes time for the body to settle down to normal. Various unpleasant symptoms may result. Hot flushes, due to excess of one particular hormone, are often troublesome. There may be some weight gain although this is due to decreased physical activity and enjoyment of sweet food rather than to true glandular effects. Minor mental upsets may occur. Depression is common at the menopause and if it does not seem to improve with plenty of company and activity see your doctor in case depression treatment is indicated. Migraines may also begin at this time (*see* MIGRAINE) but fortunately there are many forms of help for this.

By the menopause the woman's family has often grown up and left home and she may feel that she is leading a rather empty life. Now is the time to think of taking up a job, outdoor sport, voluntary work – anything to take your mind off yourself and return to happier living, for you may well have half your life to live.

175

At a more serious physical level there is loss of calcium from the bones in post-menopausal women; think how common wrist fractures are in older women. (*See* OSTEOPOROSIS.)

A few, but not all, women lose interest in sex at the menopause; if people want their sex life to continue longer it seems that those who retain the greatest interest in the subject find that helps greatly. Problems may be due partly to vaginal dryness (easily put right by KY Jelly). The vaginal lining also becomes more delicate and easily inflamed after the menopause. Some women may benefit from the *occasional* use of oestrogen cream to cope with this.

Oral oestrogen replacement (HRT) may help some if not all of the symptoms mentioned. The oestrogens must be given cyclically as in a normal period cycle and they must be combined with a progestogen which allows a regular monthly 'period' to shed any tissue which may have been building up in the uterus. Some women are reluctant to return to a monthly 'period'; others with a strong family history of heart or artery disease or who have had a deep vein thrombosis themselves or who have marked varicose veins would be ill advised to take oestrogens.

However, for some with crippling hot flushes, oestrogen replacement has given worthwhile improvement. It also prevents loss of calcium from the bones. If you are having *distressing* symptoms with the menopause see your doctor who should be able to help one way or another.

Menorrhagia

The term for heavy periods in women – often known as *flooding*. A normal period should not exceed six days (usually three to five). There should also be no clots. Menorrhagia is a sign of something wrong in the womb or the body's hormone balance. It may be due to fibroids which sometimes grow in the muscle of the womb (*see* FIBROIDS) or it may be a symptom of womb infection or the menopause. It also occurs with some blood disorders, anaemia for instance and in myxoedema (*see* MYXOEDEMA, GOITRE). In some girls the periods are heavy following their commencement at puberty, but the condition usually settles to normal within a year. If allowed to continue over a number of months, excessive blood loss may lead to iron deficiency anaemia, so medical advice should *always* be sought. Most women know what their normal loss should be, and if this increases they should consult their doctor if a month on iron tablets does not help.

Menstruation
A monthly discharge of blood-stained fluid from the womb – known as the period. The womb lining undergoes a continuous cycle of changes as a result of hormones produced by the ovary. It is gradually built up, and becomes thickened, ready to receive a fertilised ovum but if conception does not take place this lining disintegrates leading to the blood-stained loss. Usually a cycle takes about 28 days, so that the periods should occur at this interval. In some they are painless, but often there is a little pain in the low abdomen and some backache, especially the first day. Sometimes considerable pain is felt, known as dysmenorrhoea (*see* DYSMENORRHOEA) and this calls for medical advice. External sanitary pads can be worn to absorb the flow but many women of all ages prefer the convenience of a tampon designed to fit inside the vagina. They come in different sizes and the smallest will fit easily through the hymen of almost any young girl. They expand snugly in the vaginal space and cannot 'get lost' or float about the body.

Some girls start their periods at ten or eleven – others not until sixteen or seventeen. If there is no sign of a period by sixteen, have a word with your doctor. Usually it is just a case of patience but occasionally there are minor disorders that can be put right (e.g. an imperforate hymen).

All indoor and outdoor activities should be carried on as normal during menstruation and it is not an excuse for a rest from gymnastics or hockey.

If conception occurs, the lining does not break up, and therefore the periods stop.

Mental Illness

One person in seven in the UK is expected to suffer some form of mental illness in their lives and hundreds of thousands will attempt suicide, mostly unsuccessfully.

Subnormal intelligence, autism, senility and disorders arising from bodily causes like accidents, tumours, brain damage, etc., are not covered here.

As in physical illness, the disorder can vary from the trivial and tolerable to the distressing and debilitating. In a relatively mild illness where the patient has good insight into his condition, it is known as a *neurosis*. A severe illness in which the patient may have no insight into the absurdity of some of his thoughts (e.g. he has lost touch with reality) is known as a *psychosis*. This requires urgent specialist treatment.

Although an illness may be diagnosed, for example, as depression or anxiety, there may be a mixture of several conditions present. For instance a phobia, which is an irrational fear, may occur by itself or as one feature of a more extensive illness.

Symptoms of mental illness are legion, and include feelings of apathy, depression, anxiety, and obsessions, compulsions, phobias, delusions, undue excitement or verbal or physical aggression (due to fear or guilt), etc. A *phobia* or irrational fear may relate to an open space (agoraphobia), confined spaces (claustrophobia), darkness, certain animals, etc. *Obsessed* subjects find their minds compelled unhealthily to circulate on one topic. Patients can deteriorate, and develop *delusions* (see also HALLUCINATION), perhaps believing for example that they will grow a third set of teeth. Where normal fears of inflation, bombs and war, being raped etc. blow up to irrational size, this could be described as an *anxiety state*.

Depression is common, victims seeing no light at the end of the tunnel, and perhaps sitting around in misery. Symptoms can include inability to cope, lack of sense of humour, slow thinking, indecisiveness, lack of normal spontaneous behaviour, sleep disturbance and feelings of unworthiness. *The danger of this is that it can lead to thoughts of suicide*, and so urgent medical attention is needed. The depressed in the UK can also ring *The Samaritans* (number in local phone book) who treat everything in complete confidence.

Causes of Mental Illness

Stress or pressure is a common precipitant. We say 'He blew his top', which indicates prolonged breaking of health rules; e.g. too much work, play or perhaps both. Unemployment may cause fear, etc., as does ceaseless worry about insoluble problems and *guilt feelings*. *Conflict* about conscience-squaring behaviour is common as are fears over broken love-lives, and *inferiority feelings*. Sex difficulties can be serious as may be temporary upsets due to menopause or operation.

Hormone imbalance (e.g. the menopause), real or *imagined* physical illnesses, can distort the mind. Money problems, bereavement, frustration, jealousy, loneliness, etc., may harm the mental function. Nightmares, headaches, exhaustion, poor concentration, long silences, self-pity are warning smoke-signals.

Lack of space does not allow details of serious mental illnesses, but there are many excellent books on the subject.

The best preventive of mental illness is a secure loving home in childhood and an ability to understand one's difficulties and patterns of behaviour which may

179

cause conflict, stress and depression.

Migraine

A condition in which the patient suffers recurrent severe headaches. These often run in families. The attacks vary from three or four a year to one a week. In migraine the blood vessels to the brain constrict and then dilate. During constriction at the beginning of an attack, the patient sees flashes, or coloured shapes, and following this is a severe headache, often confined to one half of the head and face. The period of pain corresponds to the period of dilatation of the blood vessels. Vomiting not infrequently occurs at the height of an attack, which usually lasts for from 24 to 48 hours. If the migraine persists, the patient is usually best in bed. Sometimes elimination of articles such as cheese, chocolate, oranges and red wine from the diet will effect a cure but often it is difficult to pinpoint the offending item. Aspirin or Paracetamol may help or stronger treatments can be prescribed by the doctor. There are tablets which may reduce the incidence of attacks but these need to be taken regularly. Medical advice is needed by frequent sufferers.

Miscarriage
(*See* ABORTION, BIRTH.)

Mole
(*See* MELANOMA.)

Mongolism *(Down's Syndrome)*
A term used to describe a disorder due to the presence of an extra chromosome in the nuclei of all the body cells. (Chromosomes are coiled threads present in the centre of all body cells and bearing the genes which determine our hereditary characteristics.) The patient has slanting eyes and other physical signs which make the condition easily diagnosed at birth. There is some

associated mental retardation but mongols generally are lovable children who can fit well into their family background. After special education they can usually work in sheltered workshops. About twenty per cent are also born with a heart defect which may be correctable by heart surgery.

The extra chromosome in Down's Syndrome can occur in two ways. With increasing age the incidence amongst live births also increases so that after the age of 35 it is thought that the age of the egg is responsible. It is for this reason that amniocentesis is carried out (*see* AMNIOCENTESIS). Young mothers who have mongol babies are generally found on testing to 'carry' the extra chromosome attached to the normal one in all their body cells; they suffer no ill effects from this themselves. The young mothers run a risk of having further mongol children although this can be more precisely determined by tests in a genetic counselling clinic. Your family doctor will refer you if necessary.

Mouth Breathing
(*See* ADENOIDS.)

Multiple Sclerosis
A disease of the nervous system in which patches of the protective covering of nerve fibres are worn away piecemeal. The cause is not definitely known. It affects adults of both sexes and the course is variable. It may start with a temporary defect of vision or pins and needles in one limb. The symptoms tend to improve considerably at first and may be very few and infrequent. Some sufferers have remarkably little disability other than a little clumsiness and weakness after many years. Others follow a more rapidly progressive course and become gradually paraplegic, relying on wheelchairs. Even so, periods of improvement can occur. The arm movements tend to be retained. There is no cure yet but various symptomatic treatments are used.

Physiotherapy helps patients to make the most of their good muscles which must be kept as active as possible.

Newly diagnosed patients can take heart that they may have one of the slow forms of the illness in which serious disabilities may not happen for thirty years or more. Research into causes and treatment continues.

Mumps (*See also* ORCHITIS.)
One of the acute infections of childhood, caused by a virus, which affects the salivary glands. These glands produce saliva, and are situated in the neck, one beneath each ear and two under the chin two inches or so from the midline on either side. The glands most often affected are beneath the ears, and pain, particularly on chewing, is often the first symptom. There is usually fever, and after a day or two the glands become swollen. Both sides may be affected together, or often one side first to be followed by the other a day or so later. The incubation period of the infection – the interval between contact and the disease developing – is two to three weeks. The swelling lasts two to five days, and the patient should be kept apart from others (particularly from young men who may develop testicular inflammation) until the swelling has completely gone. He is best given a very soft diet during the early stages since chewing is often painful.

Occasionally other glands are affected, including the sex glands. In males the testes may become swollen, a condition known as *orchitis*. This very rarely results in sterility. In the UK all children are now offered immunisation during the second year.

Murmur (*See also* HEART DISEASE.)
Extra sound heard in addition to the normal 'lub-dub' of heart beats. In children this is often of no significance so parents should be reassured if the doctor is satisfied about this. Special tests can be performed if there is any doubt about the cause and the very few

found to have heart defects can usually be treated very successfully.

Muscular Dystrophy
A group of hereditary disorders in which the muscles gradually become weaker due to a defect in metabolism. There are different forms but one common type affects mainly boys in the first five years of life. The condition progresses so that eventually the child is confined to a wheelchair and rarely lives beyond twenty as the breathing muscles are involved. Milder forms of dystrophy occur. Research is going on into the cause and treatments. At present physiotherapy is the mainstay of treatment. Young couples with a family history of muscular dystrophy should have genetic counselling as to the precise risks. Ask your doctor about this. An expectant mother from an 'at risk' family can have a test done at the fifteenth week of pregnancy to establish the sex of the baby. If it is a boy there is an even chance of his being affected and she may wish to have termination of pregnancy. A girl will not be affected but can 'carry' the disorder. Recent gene research is heralding prevention of some forms of this distressing condition.

Muscular Rheumatism *(includes fibrositis)*
A vague term used to describe various aches and pains in muscles and soft tissues and due to a variety of causes. Most cases are associated with minor degrees of arthritis or ligament strain in nearby joints – such as the neck, shoulders, hips and knee. The pain is felt in the fleshy muscular area rather than in the deeper ligaments and bones. Others are due to chronic strain as in the lumbar muscles following gardening – lumbago. Rheumatism due to over-use of the muscles needs a short rest, plenty of heat and two aspirins or Paracetamols three times a day. Rheumatism due to chronic conditions in joint and ligaments needs as much

mobility brought to the area as possible. Rubbing with liniment is helpful. Keep all the joints moving and keep active in general. Soluble aspirin or Paracetamol and an appropriate support pad such as a Seton Arthro-pad will allow all the movement to continue with great benefit all round. Supports are not intended for permanent use as they could weaken muscles – wear for a few days while pain is severe. (*See* ARTHRITIS.)

A very important form of rheumatism is *polymyalgia rheumatica*. Symptoms are dramatic and prompt treatment is required. An elderly lady finds that her upper arms and thighs become so stiff and painful that she can hardly move and may be literally 'stuck' on a chair. There is often no history of previous 'rheumatism' or 'arthritis'. She needs a doctor urgently as blood tests will prove the diagnosis and the need for treatment with steroids. Treatment is needed for six months to a year – not less – and the condition rapidly improves.

Myalgic Encephalomyelitis (ME)
See POST-VIRAL FATIGUE SYNDROME.

Myasthenia Gravis
The name of an uncommon disease, in which the messages from the brain to various muscles are not properly passed on, so that the muscles affected become weak. The face is often involved, so that the eyelids droop and the patient is unable to laugh or smile. The cause is a fault at the junction between the muscle and nerve which becomes blocked to the 'chemical messenger', which ought to stimulate it, causing the muscles to move. Treatment consists of giving 'excess chemical messenger' to overcome the block. This often results in a great improvement; in other cases a cure may be brought about by an operation on a gland in the chest called the *thymus* which is not working properly in this disease.

Myocarditis

Inflammation of the heart muscle. It may complicate several virus diseases, and often accompanies an attack of rheumatic fever. (*See* HEART DISEASE *and* RHEUMATIC FEVER.)

Myxoedema

A disorder of the thyroid gland where there is insufficient secretion of thyroid hormone (thyroxine). The body becomes sluggish, and there is increase in fat. The hair becomes coarse, the mental processes slow and the skin dry and scaly. In women, heavy periods and anaemia may occur. It can be cured by Thyroxine tablets which have to be taken permanently. (*See* GOITRE.)

N

Naevus
(*See* BIRTHMARK.)

Nails
Nails are often affected by the general health, and fragile nails can indicate anaemia. After a serious illness ridges may appear, which grow out as health returns.

Nail Biting
Nail biting is often a distressing nervous habit in children. Scolding usually has little effect since the habit is mostly instinctive. Punishment upsets the child further so that nail biting becomes more and not less pronounced. The nails should be kept short so that there is little encouragement to bite them. It is best not to make too much of the matter, as the habit is nearly always one which the child grows out of, especially if success is rewarded.

Nail Discolouration
This may occur in certain skin diseases such as Psoriasis or Fungal Infections.

Nephritis
The medical term for inflammation of the kidneys. It may occur as an acute condition (*see* ACUTE) when recovery is often complete, but sometimes the disease becomes chronic and lowers the general health considerably. The reader should consult the article on KIDNEY DISEASES.

Nettlerash (*Urticaria*)

One of the allergic diseases (*see* ALLERGY, HAY FEVER). It is due to irritation of the skin by some foreign substance – often in the diet. Red weals develop on the skin which irritate, and have white tops. One common cause of urticaria is eating shellfish, and sometimes, especially in children, eggs or certain fruits may cause the condition. The rash does not usually last long, and the best treatment is to avoid the substance which causes the attack. Calamine lotion is soothing, and antihistamine tablets cure rapidly. Some of the newer ones such as Triludan do not cause drowsiness.

Neuralgia

(*See* NEURITIS.)

Neuritis

Inflammation of a nerve. It may occur when a nerve passes through inflamed tissue or when a nerve is compressed as in sciatica (*see* SCIATICA). Certain metallic poisons such as lead, which may contaminate drinking water, are capable of setting up a neuritis. It can also be due to virus infection and in multiple sclerosis (*see* MULTIPLE SCLEROSIS) many widespread areas of neuritis occur.

There are two sorts of nerves – those which carry sensations (pain, etc.) back to the brain, and those which carry messages to move the muscles. In neuritis, both functions may be disturbed, so that the muscles in the affected part become weak, and sensations disturbed, resulting in pain, numbness or sometimes 'pins and needles'. The condition is often confused with *neuralgia* which is the occurrence of pain in the area served by a particular nerve. The condition is often due to an 'over-flow', so to speak, from a small painful focus. Thus a diseased tooth may set up neuralgia of the whole face. The pain from neuralgia can often be lessened by aspirin or Paracetamol, but it is always wisest to see a doctor for face or temple pain as often there is some underlying cause to be put right before the trouble will settle completely. Neuritis is sometimes confused with ARTERITIS.

Night Blindness
The sensitive part at the back of the eye (the retina) has two components – one for day vision, including colours; the other for vision at night, where there is no appreciation of colour; only of shade and shape. The efficient working of the latter depends upon a good supply of vitamin A. If this is lacking in diet, night blindness may result.

Night Sweats
Excessive sweating at night is often a sign of a raised temperature and can be caused by a variety of conditions. Infections such as tooth abscesses and sinusitis are probably the commonest. Night sweats also occur in thyrotoxicosis (*see* GOITRE) and in anxiety states. Although much rarer nowadays TUBERCULOSIS is an important cause. *Recurrent* night sweats should be reported to your doctor for investigation.

Nit
(*See* LICE.)

Nose Bleeding
(*See* HAEMORRHAGE.)

NSU (*Non-Specific Urethritis, Non-Specific Genital Infection*)
Any inflammation of the urethra (outlet from the bladder) in which have been excluded such diseases as GONORRHOEA, SYPHILIS and infection (*see* VAGINITIS) by larger germs such as trichomonas and monilia (thrush).

It is now the commonest venereal disease in the UK. Symptoms may include pain on passing water, soreness of the parts and discharge, but are milder than in gonorrhoea and the symptoms are usually completely absent in the female. About fifty per cent of NSU cases are thought to be caused by a virus-like germ called chlamydia. Unfortunately chlamydia can cause serious infection in the eyes of newborn babies, as can gonorrhoea.

Treatment is not perfect but consists of tetracycline antibiotics for four to six weeks. This is different from the usual treatments for *cystitis* (a different illness) so any patient who suspects that pain on passing water may be due to sexual contact should always mention this to his or her doctor or attend a special clinic. In spite of treatment a few men develop serious complications such as arthritis and inflammation of the eyes and it is not absolutely certain the treatment of female contacts will prevent development of eye inflammation in new-born babies.

The only definite way to avoid these ills is not to have casual sex where you cannot be sure that your partner is free of infection.

Nuclear Magnetic Resonance (NMR)
A recent medical invention which allows magnetic rays to be used in a similar way to sound waves and X rays to investigate the structure of certain body organs.

Nystagmus
The name of a condition in which there is a rapid to and fro movement of the eyeballs. It can be seen in normal persons who have spun round until giddy and it usually passes off in less than a minute. Sometimes, in disease of the brain, or in people who have worked long in a poor light, like miners, the control of the eye movements becomes disturbed so that nystagmus occurs all the time. In modern well-lit mines this should no longer occur. Some families have a tendency to this condition for no obvious reason and their sight is not impaired.

Your doctor will advise you if any abnormal eye movements you may have noted are of any serious significance.

O

Obesity

Excessive weight is unsightly and detrimental to the health as it imposes unnecessary strain on the body. In a few cases, the condition may be due to a glandular disorder.

Usually, however, the cause boils down to mathematics. Too much fat-producing food, too little exercise to burn it up, so the fat accumulates. Unfortunately some people burn up their food at a slower rate than others and do have to eat a much more restricted diet to achieve a reasonable weight. In spite of treatments which are advertised, there is no safe, easy road to weight reduction. The key is to restrict fat-producing foods so that no more fat is stored, and what has become stored is burnt up. The chief offenders are fat and sugary foods which become converted to fat if not used. Sugar, sweets, jams and pastry must be reduced to a minimum by anyone wishing to lose weight. Fish, green vegetables and fruit may be eaten *ad lib*. Meat should be lean and not exceed 6 oz (150g) daily, and butter, margarine and milk should be restricted. Cheese and eggs may be substituted for meat and fish.

Do not be tempted to 'nibble' between meals. The more daily exercise taken, within reason, the better, as this helps to burn the fat already accumulated. Obesity is a long-term problem which requires a long-term solution. Two or three weeks 'dieting' is useless. A complete and permanent change in dietary and exercise habits is needed. Do not ask your doctor for 'slimming' tablets. The only ones available cut down your appetite; they do not 'slim' you and their effect tends to wear off.

Contrary to popular belief, excess fluid is not a cause of overweight. Except in serious disease even the most bloated of us is only carrying about seven pounds too much fluid but probably about three stone too much fat. Most of the excess fluid will disappear along with the fat if you stick to the above diet, as long as salt intake is kept to a minimum (a little in cooking only). It is no good 'starving' as the bowel needs volume to help the 'fat stuff' to pass. Eat lots of fruits and vegetables to provide the fibre needed to keep the bowels right. *See* HEALTHY EATING, *page 11*.

Obstruction
Term commonly used in relation to the bowel when blockage by strangulation within a hernia (rupture), tumour, or adhesions from a previous operation, causes intense pain due to the increased efforts of the bowel muscle to expel the cause of the block. There is usually constipation, and vomiting develops as the intestinal contents build up behind the source of the obstruction. Treatment is usually by emergency operation to remove the obstructions. The combination of severe abdominal pain, constipation and vomiting requires urgent medical help.

In elderly people extreme constipation can lead to this condition and treatment is by bowel washouts (enema) and changing the diet.

Oedema
Collection of fluid within the body tissues. (Sometimes archaically called dropsy.) Due to gravity, the lower parts of the body are those most affected, so that ankles, then legs, and later the abdomen become distended. Swollen legs will show a little pit when pressed with the finger. There are various causes. It may be associated with HEART DISEASE when circulation

becomes so sluggish that fluid leaks from the blood vessels into the tissues. It can be due to KIDNEY DISEASE, when the kidneys are unable to eliminate excess water which accumulates. Some degree of swelling of the ankles especially after middle age is common and does not necessarily indicate serious illness. Overweight is a common and remediable cause. In pregnancy some women develop swollen ankles. Treatment of oedema includes rest, restriction of salt (which 'holds onto' the fluid) and the use of tablets or injections to eliminate water (diuretics).

Old Age
If one lives long enough mind and body deteriorate but probably the way to prolong happy living is, as far as possible, never to think of your age *in years* at all.

It may be that those who are optimistic and do not adopt the attitude that they have to give up things, or stay in, because it is 'too wet or cold' remain healthiest. *Keep exercising mind and body* and develop interests to compensate for those which have to be given up. If you cannot play tennis at 60 consider bowls, rambling, etc. Never think: 'I must not buy a coat as I may not need it'. *That*, is the philosophy of death. Every age has its compensations and many people in their 90s still enjoy life. With modern medicines there is much that can be done to delay the effects of age and reduce the risk that you may have to enter hospital. The ability to adjust *physically and mentally* is probably the most likely way to hit a century. To all who say 'I do not want to live that long,' a good reply is, 'if you do, you will'.

Onchocerciasis (*See also* FILARIASIS.)
An infection with a filarial worm found in Africa, Central and South America which is transmitted by flies. It causes infection of various parts of the eye causing blindness.

Operations
(*See* ANAESTHESIA.)

Orchitis
Inflammation of the testes, the male sex glands. It usually results from an attack by germs and may occur as a complication of mumps. Another cause is a venereal infection, especially gonorrhoea. The symptoms are pain and swelling in the testes, and if these occur there should be no time lost in seeing a doctor. In a young male swelling and pain can be due to twisting of the testicle (*see* TORSION OF TESTIS) and urgent operation is required to save the testis. Men who suffer orchitis – a rather frightening illness – should not be too afraid. The enormous swelling of the testis can be helped by various drugs and normally the gland returns to its usual function without any loss of virility or fertility.

Osteoarthritis
The 'wear and tear' type of arthritis in which the joint surfaces become roughened, irregular and painful. It may be aggravated by excess weight or previous injury and is common in the weight-bearing joints such as the spine, hip and knee. For treatment see ARTHRITIS.

Osteomyelitis (*Bone Infection*)
Infection within the bone cavity. Germs from some focus of infection which may not be obvious may, particularly after injury, gain entry to the blood stream and thence to the interior of a bone. The condition most commonly occurs in the knee, towards the ends of the bones above or below the joint, but can occur in any other bones. The infection, trapped within the bones, causes excruciating pain and a high temperature. Attempts to move the affected part increases the pain and the child (for children are usually affected) will remain unusually still. Antibiotics may cure but sometimes it is necessary to operate to release the pus. Occasionally the tubercle bacillus is the cause and it is

194

then known as tuberculous osteomyelitis. Treatment in this case requires anti-tuberculous drugs which are very effective. Antibiotics have largely prevented the long-term effects which included destruction of large areas of bone and recurrences of discharge from sinuses in the limbs but the condition still needs urgent treatment in the early stages. Probably the commonest cause is bone infection after penetrating or crush injuries following accidents.

Osteoporosis
Thinning of the bones which occurs with increasing age, especially in women immediately after the menopause. Wrist, hip and spine fractures become common.

Hormone replacement therapy helps to prevent osteoporosis. A good intake of calcium and vitamin D is recommended, although their effect in preventing osteoporosis is debatable.

Otitis Externa
Inflammation of the outer ear canal leading down to the eardrum. It causes itching, pain and discharge. Treatment is by eardrops which soothe and contain antibioitic or antifungus agents. It commonly follows immersion under water with poor drying of the ears. You will need medical advice.

Otitis Media
Inflammation of the middle ear usually due to infection which has spread from the nose or throat. EARACHE, especially in children, is frequently due to otitis media and early medical attention is needed so that antibiotics can be prescribed if necessary. In this way complications like MASTOIDITIS, chronic discharge and DEAFNESS may be avoided.

Otorrhoea
Discharge from the ear. It often occurs in OTITIS EXTERNA

and also in OTITIS MEDIA if the eardrum has burst due to pressure from pus building up in the middle ear. This type of drum perforation usually heals quickly, but in neglected cases the perforation may be permanent and the discharge recur from time to time. Such sufferers can be helped by surgical treatment. (*See* DEAFNESS.)

Ovarian Cyst
A fluid-filled swelling which can develop in one or both ovaries. There may be no symptoms unless it becomes twisted to cause pain. Cysts may sometimes cause irregular periods and the 'chocolate' cysts of ENDOME-TRIOSIS are associated with painful periods. Sometimes cysts are only noticed when they become large enough to cause an increase in girth. An ovarian cyst requires medical investigation as occasionally it may contain a tumour. (*See* DYSMENORRHOEA.)

Ovaries
The female sex glands, which lie inside the abdominal cavity, one on each side above the womb. They produce the ova, or eggs, which after uniting with a sperm, are capable of growing into a baby. One ovum is usually produced approximately every 28 days, about midway between the times of the periods, and the lining of the womb is increased in thickness to receive it. (*See* GLANDS, HORMONES, INFERTILITY, MENOPAUSE, MENSTRUATION.)

P

Pacemaker
An artificial device fitted to regulate the heartbeat when the normal rhythm is lost. (*See* HEART DISEASE.)

Pain
A warning signal. The body is supplied with a network of nerves which carry messages to the brain, and when these are irritated or injured we feel pain. Pain lets us know something is wrong, and serves to protect the injured or diseased part from further damage since a painful part is usually moved as little as possible. In injury the body may not wait for the brain to analyse the message before taking action. We have all had the experience of touching something hot and feeling the sudden jerk as the hand jumps away almost before the pain is felt. This is brought about by the spinal cord where the pain signals are 'short-circuited' as it were and made to move the muscles *before* they reach the brain. This is known as a *reflex*, and may occur even when a person is unconscious. Blinking when something approaches the eye is example of a reflex. Whatever its nature, pain is an indication of something amiss. It may be only trivial, and we all suffer from aches and pains which do not last long. Any severe pain, or any which is persistent, should not be ignored. See your doctor and get him to treat you.

Pallor
Pronounced paleness or pallor may simply be a matter of complexion or may indicate a shortage of the red

colouring matter (haemoglobin) in the blood. The latter is more likely if the lips and red membrane inside the eyelids are also pale. (*See* ANAEMIA.)

Palpitations
Normally the heart beats steadily and we are unaware of its action. Sometimes when the beating becomes quicker or irregular we are aware of a fluttering sensation in the chest known as palpitations. It occasionally occurs in heart disease and thyrotoxicosis (*see* GOITRE) when the heart is working less well than normal. Usually palpitations are not due to any serious disorder. They often accompany an emotional upset, and can be brought on by excess cigarette smoking or drinking excess tea or coffee. Lay people are often unduly worried by palpitations and feel something serious has gone wrong. If the symptom persists for any time medical advice should certainly be sought, but in most cases there is no cause for anxiety. Worry and stress make us unduly aware of the *normal* action of the heart as well as tending to speed it up. This is the commonest cause of palpitations. If the doctor tells you all is well, do not worry about the condition. (*See* PULSE.)

Pancreas
An organ lying behind the stomach. It produces digestive juices which pass along a duct into the duodenum. Small areas of its surface (islets) produce insulin which is poured directly into the blood stream to control the level of blood sugar.

Pancreatitis
This is a condition when the pancreas becomes inflamed producing very severe abdominal pain. This condition often follows drinking an excess amount of alcohol. Mild attacks respond to rest and fluids but severe attacks may require an operation.

Paralysis

The loss of voluntary movement of a part of the body – a loss of the power to move the muscles concerned. It may be associated with a loss or disorder of sensation, but this is not necessarily the case since the two sets of nerves, motor and sensory, are separate (*see* NEURITIS). Paralysis may be a symptom of disease or injury to that part of the brain, which controls movements (e.g. a STROKE), to the spinal cord which passes on the messages, or to the nerves themselves (e.g. NEURITIS). (One of the commonest causes of spinal paralysis nowadays follows injury to the spine due to motorcycle or car accidents.) Unfortunately, most types of paralysis (except where due to fear, when it is fleeting) which have persisted for any length of time do not usually recover completely, because injured nerve cells cannot be replaced. However, there is often some remaining function in the part concerned, and by special exercises designed to make use of this the patient can often do much to overcome the disability.

Paranoia

A type of mental illness, characterised by suspicion of being victimised. It may develop quickly or slowly and may persist or remit. One cause of the illness could be loneliness. The patient tends to brood a lot. Mild cases may merely be considered eccentric or bad tempered people. By the time a doctor is seen, a sufferer may, in rare cases, be deluded enough to believe that God has chosen him to do something, possibly something terrible. It can be difficult but *essential* to get the patient to see a doctor. So tenacious can the patient's views be that some of those close to him may imagine them correct. Specialist treatment is often required.

In the early stages, various modern drug treatments of one kind or another are often useful, and may need to be continued for some time. Psychotherapy may be of use later on. The outlook should be excellent if a doctor can be found of an acceptable wavelength to the patient. A new job or improved life conditions may be advisable. (*See* ELECTRO CONVULSIVE THERAPY, MANIA, MENTAL ILLNESS *and* SCHIZOPHRENIA.)

Parasite
A plant or animal which lives upon or within another living organism causing damage and giving no benefit. Examples of parasitic diseases are malaria (*see* MALARIA) in which the parasite is transferred from mosquito to man, and amoebic dysentery (*see* DYSENTERY) in which the parasite is acquired from contaminated food or water.

Parathyroids
Four small glands arranged in two pairs near the outer lobes of the thyroid gland in the neck. They produce a hormone which controls calcium metabolism and thus the condition of bones. Too much hormone, e.g. with a tumour of the gland, eventually produces kidney and bone damage. Too little hormone causes defects in teeth, nails, skin and hair and can also cause an acute form of muscular cramp plus pins and needles, known as tetany.

Parkinson's Disease (*Paralysis Agitans, shaking palsy*)
A condition in which the muscles become stiff and jerky in their action. It is due to disturbance of that part of the brain which controls the smooth working of muscles, caused in some cases by hardening of the cerebral arteries. Sufferers are greatly handicapped by the stiffness and tremor, but can often be helped by medicines which help to lessen these symptoms. A breakthrough in treatment was the development of the drug 'Levo-dopa' which has been of great value to many. Rarely found in the under-fifties.

Parturition (*Medical term for child-birth*)
(*See* BIRTH.)

Penicillin
This very important drug was discovered by Sir Alexander Fleming at St Mary's Hospital, London when a mould got into a dish in which bacteria were growing. It was noted at the time that the bacteria were killed by this mould but it was some years before the active ingredient – penicillin – was extracted in sufficient quantity to become the first of the antibiotics (*see* ANTIBIOTICS). Unlike many powerful drugs penicillin is harmless to normal body tissues except in a few patients who are, or become, allergic to it. Mild allergy usually consists of a skin rash, and anyone who has had this should avoid future doses of penicillin (there are now alternative antibiotics).

Penis
The male sex organ, containing a canal, the *urethra*, through which urine from the bladder is passed. If this becomes inflamed, as for instance in GONORRHOEA, the condition is known as urethritis. Normally the penis is relaxed, but it contains a special tissue in which are large blood spaces. Under the influence of sexual excitement or sometimes friction these become distended with blood which causes the organ to erect and become stiff. At the end of the sexual act, semen, a fluid containing the male sperms (seed), is discharged via the urethra. Rarely, sexual union is made difficult by a deformity of the penis. The opening at the end of the urethra may lie on the under-surface of the penis (hypospadias) or sometimes the organ is bent over. Successful surgical refashioning or reshaping is now usually performed in the early years of life and can cure or help in many instances. (*See* BALANITIS, CIRCUMCISION *and* PHIMOSIS.)

Pericarditis

The heart is surrounded by a membrane known as the pericardium. Under some circumstances this may become inflamed. There are many causes and the commonest is a range of virus infections. The inflamed membrane may pour out fluid which then collects around the heart, a condition known as *pericardial effusion*. Whatever the cause the condition is serious, and the patient requires immediate treatment in a specialised unit.

Period

(*See* AMENORRHOEA, BIRTH, MENSTRUATION.)

Peritonitis

Inflammation of the membrane (peritoneum) which lines the abdominal cavity. It is a very serious condition and usually occurs when an infected organ bursts as in APPENDICITIS. Treatment depends on the cause but often includes emergency operation as well as antibiotics. Prevention means treatment of the original trouble (e.g. appendicitis) before this stage is reached. We all get odd tummy aches from time to time but in general any abdominal pain which persists for four hours, especially if there is associated fever and vomiting, needs a doctor's attention. The pain of peritonitis is often so severe that it causes collapse in such cases; if a doctor cannot be immediately located, dial 999 for an emergency ambulance (in UK).

Pernicious Anaemia

Study the article on ANAEMIA in general. Whereas many anaemias are due to lack of iron, pernicious anaemia is due to lack of vitamin B_{12}, also essential for the manufacture of red blood cells. It is caused by poor absorption from the stomach rather than inadequate diet and occurs in older people where the stomach lining has become thin and unable to deal with this vitamin.

Lack of vitamin B_{12} (cyanocobalamin) also causes damage to nerve cells so that as well as symptoms of anaemia (tiredness, shortness of breath, etc.) the patient may have disturbances of sensation (pins and needles, numbness, etc.) and weakness of the arms and legs. As the patient is unable to absorb vitamin B_{12} from the stomach, treatment is by regular injection. When the condition is first diagnosed injections may be given several times a week. However, after the first week or two they can be reduced to once monthly and after a year to three monthly.

A similar condition arises if the diet is deficient in vitamin B_{12} (rare in the West) or after surgery for peptic ulcer when a part of the stomach is removed. Increased intake of liver is indicated for the former and regular injections of B_{12} for the latter.

Pessary
Any device placed in the vagina for the purposes of treatment. It may be to support the uterus as in prolapse (*see* PROLAPSE) or to act as a contraceptive (diaphragm pessary) or to treat infection when it can consist of a drug incorporated in a suitably shaped soluble tablet.

Pharyngitis
Inflammation of the throat often accompanying TONSIL-LITIS or (if the tonsils have been removed) occurring alone. It may be caused by the streptococcus – the 'tonsillitis germ' – or by numerous viruses. Only 'strep' throats respond to penicillin. The vast majority of virus-inflamed throats settle in their own good time (about a week) and can be soothed by gargle or glycerine of thymol and soluble aspirin.

Phimosis (*See also* BALANITIS *and* CIRCUMCISION.)
A constriction of the male foreskin. Normally after the age of three it can be pulled back to expose the tip of

the penis for purposes of hygiene but sometimes the opening of the foreskin is too narrow. Parents should not attempt to retract the foreskin before the child is ˙ʔur as scarring can occur in the delicate tissues. Slight adherence of the foreskin in a young boy can often be treated medically by gentle stretching. Where there is genuine phimosis it is usually best to deal with this condition by circumcision, since debris is likely to accumulate beneath the foreskin, resulting in inflammation (BALANITIS). Sometimes a tight foreskin becomes constricted around the head of the penis after it has been pulled back – a condition known as *paraphimosis*. For this, too, circumcision is often the best treatment.

Phlebitis

Inflammation of a vein. Veins may become inflamed as the result of disease or injury, and the most common situation is in the leg where the cause is often a varicosity of the veins (*see* VARICOSE VEINS). The vein affected becomes hard, and can be felt like a cord beneath the skin. It is often tender and the overlying skin may be inflamed. Consult a doctor, for phlebitis in a superficial vein is liable to spread if not properly treated. He will probably prescribe a supporting bandage, tablets to reduce inflammation and plenty of walking exercise to keep the circulation flowing through the deeper veins of the leg. Outlook usually excellent.

Photophobia

A term applied when the eyes are unduly sensitive to light. It commonly occurs where the eyes are inflamed, and may be a feature of generalised infections in which the eyes are involved, e.g. MEASLES. It often accompanies any severe headache, and frequently occurs during an attack of MIGRAINE. Serious but less common causes are POLIOMYELITIS and MENINGITIS when it accompanies headache and neck stiffness. The treatment depends on the cause, but whatever that is, it is always best to avoid bright light and straining the eyes when they are sensitive.

Piles
(*See* HAEMORRHOIDS.)

Pink Eye
The popular name for a bacterial CONJUNCTIVITIS. (*See* EYE, EYESIGHT.)

Pins and Needles (*Paraethesiae*)
Sensations such as burning and prickling – often in the limbs. It may be due to pressure on the nerve (your arm may 'go to sleep' if you lie on it) or it may be due to inflammation as in neuritis (*see* NEURITIS). Often the pricking goes if one alters one's sleeping position to, for example, having an arm behind the back. If these sensations persist, see your doctor.

Plague
An epidemic disease once common in the West due to infection with bacillus pestis; it is spread initially by fleas on rats. It occurs in two forms: bubonic in which the glands swell 'buboes'; and pneumonic in which pneumonia occurs, and which, unless treated with antibiotics and intensive care, is frequently fatal. There is a vaccine which imparts a degree of protection.

Pleurisy
Each lung is enclosed in a double layer of thin membrane known as the pleura (*see Fig. 8, page 136*). When it becomes inflamed the condition is known as pleurisy. It is nearly always due to an invasion by germs which may reach the pleura through the bloodstream or from the lung beneath. Thus pleurisy is apt to be associated with infections of the lung – particularly

pneumonia. When the pleura becomes inflamed it often pours out fluid which collects between the two layers, and this is known as a *pleural effusion*. During the early stages, pleurisy is usually accompanied by a sharp pain in the chest on breathing, since the inflamed layers of membrane rub against each other every time a breath is taken. In the later stages, if fluid forms, the pain passes off since the fluid prevents the two layers from coming into contact. However, the presence of the fluid reduces the movement of the lung so that there is often shortness of breath.

Pleurisy is often due to a number of viruses and there may be little or no associated pneumonia. Treatment is by rest and tablets to reduce pain thus aiding deep breathing. Where pleurisy is due to bacteria it responds well to antibiotics.

Pleurodynia (*Epidemic Myalgia*)
A common virus infection (also called *Bornholm disease)* affecting the muscles between the ribs and sometimes causing true pleurisy and pericarditis. Slight fever and a sharp chest pain are the main symptoms and it occurs in epidemics often in young people. (*See* PLEURISY.)

Pneumoconiosis
Disease of the lungs in which inhalation of dust causes thickening and scarring in the delicate lung tissues. It used to be an occupational hazard in mining before the introduction of safety measures such as air filters. The end result is persistent shortness of breath and liability to chest infections and other lung disease. Similar reactions occur with exposure to silicon (silicosis) – a hazard among knife grinders – and to *blue* asbestos now banned by most companies (asbestosis).

Pneumonia
A serious infection of part of the lung causing the

normally 'spongy' tissue to become solid. There are several varieties of pneumonia depending upon the germ and the parts of the lung affected. Thus *lobar pneumonia* is due to the pneumococcus, which attacks a whole lobe of the lung at once. In BRONCHO-PNEUMONIA, which may be caused by different germs, the infection is more scattered and occurs in patches surrounding the breathing tubes. It follows some other respiratory infection, such as a cold or 'flu, when the patient, instead of recovering, grows worse. There is a pain in the chest if the pleura is involved (*see* PLEURISY), usually a high temperature of 103°F (39½°C) and a cough productive of rusty-looking phlegm. As more of the lung becomes involved, some shortness of breath becomes apparent. There may be a tinge of blueness in face and lips.

A type of pneumonia increasing in frequency is that due to Legionnaires' Disease (*see* LEGIONNAIRES' DISEASE).

Most forms of pneumonia respond rapidly to anti-biotic treatment but pneumonias sometimes fail to respond to such treatment and such patients require intensive hospital care, including oxygen and venti-lation.

Pneumothorax
The term for the presence of air between the layers of the pleura (*see* PLEURISY). Sometimes, when there is disease present and sometimes for no obvious reason a small hole may form in a terminal air passage and allow air to escape, and press on the lung causing it to collapse. In most instances time alone will allow a lung to expand naturally curing the condition. Occasionally a 'tension' pneumothorax develops as air continues to build up in the chest cavity pressing ever harder on the collapsed lung. Emergency treatment in hospital is needed to release the air through a tube inserted through the chest wall. Thereafter it recovers similarly

as ordinary pneumothorax.

Occasionally the condition becomes recurrent and such cases may need an operation to 'stick' the pleural layers together (pleuradesis).

Poisoning

Many substances in daily use are harmful and may be taken accidentally, or sometimes deliberately in intended suicide. The most common symptoms are pain in mouth, throat and stomach, vomiting and collapse and undue drowsiness. Later, there is often diarrhoea. A sudden illness in a person previously well should arouse suspicion, and if the victim is questioned it may be found that something out of the ordinary has been taken. The remedy for a poison depends on its nature, but the *general* treatment is usually the same. Call the doctor and let him know that an overdose of medicine or poisoning is suspected. The treatment is very complicated and usually needs expert medical care in hospital. Many first aid procedures can be dangerous. Attempts to make a drowsy or semi-conscious patient vomit should await the arrival of a doctor since *inhalation of vomit into the lungs can easily happen.* Never give a solution of salt. If someone has taken an overdose of tablets keep the bottle to enable the doctor to identify which drug and how much has been taken. Vomited material should also be kept for inspection.

Do not give other medicines or alcohol except to the fully conscious and co-operative patients as below. Drowsiness and coma should be treated by placing the patient in the three quarters prone (i.e. lying on his side) position, making sure the tongue is pulled forwards to maintain a clear airway. Dentures should be removed. Be ready to use artificial respiration (*see* ARTIFICIAL RESPIRATION) if necessary.

(a) *Acids.* These include sulphuric acid (oil of vitriol), hydrochloric acid (spirits of salt), battery acid, nitric acid, soldering fluid, formic acid (kettle descaler) and phenol (carbolic acid). Give a glass of milk mixed with two teaspoons of bicarbonate of soda or the stomach mixture 'Asilone', four teaspoons to the fully conscious patient. Do not induce vomiting.

(b) *Alkalis*. The most common are caustics, such as caustic potash, caustic soda and ammonia. A glass of milk mixed, if possible, with beaten white of egg may be given to the conscious patient. Do not induce vomiting.

(c) *Arsenic*. This is present in sheep dip and less commonly nowadays in weedkiller. Vomiting may be induced in the conscious patient by giving two teaspoons of mustard in a glass of water. This should be followed by a glass of milk mixed with two teaspoons of vegetable oil.

(d) *Carbon tetrachloride* (dry cleaning fluid). Give nothing by mouth.

(e) *Paraquat*. This is the most dangerous of the modern weedkillers. Urgent specialist care is vital and the patient should be rushed to the nearest hospital either by emergency ambulance or home transport if quicker. Vomiting may be induced, as for Arsenic (above).

(f) *Overdose of sleeping tablets, tranquillisers or anti-depressant drugs*. If the patient is fully conscious, as may be the case within minutes of taking the overdose, induction of vomiting may be tried by two teaspoons of mustard in water. Keep the patient warm whilst awaiting medical aid and be prepared to administer artificial respiration (*see* ARTIFICIAL RESPIRATION) if necessary.

To avoid accidental poisoning, all medicines and other poisonous substances should be kept out of reach of children since they will readily eat tablets experimentally or mistake them for sweets and such substances should be kept in containers which are child-proof. Children will also drink any liquid especially foolishly transferred to a 'soft drink' bottle. This is the usual

209

reason for the accidental drinking of household cleaners, carbolic acid and paraquat. A little common sense would prevent these tragedies. Warn children not to eat any berries as it is impossible for them to distinguish the safe from the poisonous.

Poliomyelitis (*Infantile Paralysis*)
This disease is now fortunately rare in the UK and is becoming rarer throughout the world. It is infectious and caused by a virus which gains entry to the intestines via the mouth and stomach. First it produces a vague 'flu-like illness with fever, diarrhoea, headache and limb pains. After two to three days paralysis may develop in some people. As the virus reaches the spinal nerve cells controlling movement this paralysis may affect a single limb or may be extensive and affect the breathing muscles, causing death or the need for mechanically assisted respiration. Avoid exercise in the early stage of the illness as it seems to increase the extent of the subsequent paralysis so rest is vital if there is any suspicion of polio.

Fortunately the development of safe and effective oral vaccines has almost eliminated this disease from Western countries. However, in some tropical and sub-tropical countries it still occurs in small epidemics. Travellers to such countries, including the Mediterranean coast, are advised to be vaccinated or to have booster doses. There is at present a campaign to eliminate polio by a world vaccination programme.

Polycythaemia
Medical term for an uncommon condition where the red cells in the blood are increased above normal. It often causes a ruddy complexion, and may be associated with headaches, and sometimes raised blood pressure. There are medicines which can be taken by mouth to reduce the number of cells to a more normal level.

Polypus (*Polyp*)

A small, pear-shaped growth forming on the internal surfaces of the body. Polypi are usually caused by chronic infection and are commonly found in ears or nose. They also occur in women, sometimes, at the *cervix*, the exit from the womb. Polypi are not dangerous in themselves, but may cause irritation and bleed from time to time. They are usually easily removed by a small operation.

Post-Viral Fatigue Syndrome (*Myalgic Encephalo-myelitis*)

This condition follows a 'flu-like illness and may last for weeks, months or years. It is more common in women. The main symptom is extreme muscle fatigue on exercise. This may be associated with headaches, dizziness, lack of concentration, poor memory, depression and other symptoms. Clinical signs are not usually found and some patients are labelled as hypochondriacs. It may be due to a persistent viral infection but is now thought likely to be an atypical depressive illness. A self-help group – The Myalgic Encephalomyelitis Association – exists to help sufferers.

Treatment is supportive and depends on reassurance, a graduated exercise programme and counselling.

Pregnancy

Pregnancy occurs when the female ovum is fertilised by the sperm and embeds satisfactorily in the lining of the womb. The first indication is usually a stopping of the monthly period though there are other causes (*see* AMENORRHOEA). Any blood loss after pregnancy is confirmed requires medical advice. During the early months there is sometimes a feeling of sickness or vomiting in the morning. The breasts enlarge somewhat and during a first pregnancy the nipples and surrounding skin become darker. After about the third month

211

the abdomen becomes noticeably and progressively larger. The normal duration of pregnancy is nine months, or to be more precise, 40 weeks. The expected date of birth can be calculated thus. Take the first day of the last monthly period, count back three months and add seven days. Thus if the last period started on August 14th the birth would be due on May 21st. Every woman should put herself under the care of her doctor during pregnancy. It is important to have a regular check to see that all is going well, and she will require advice about diet and exercise so that she can remain in good health during pregnancy. The blood pressure needs to be taken regularly to exclude rises which might be harmful. If the blood pressure does rise and if albumen appears in the urine the mother needs complete rest, sometimes in hospital. Occasionally the birth needs to be induced early if rest does not suffice. Cigarette smoking should be given up as it damages the unborn child and is one cause of underweight babies. No medicines, other than those deemed necessary and safe by your doctor, should be taken, especially in the first three months, as they can lead to deformities of the baby. Extra iron and vitamins are advisable during pregnancy and can be prescribed by your doctor. If all is going well there is no reason why you cannot continue your job at least until the seven month stage. (*See* BIRTH, BREAST *and* INFANT FEEDING.)

Premature Birth
A birth before the 35th week and after the 24th week of pregnancy. (*See* ABORTION *and* BIRTH.)

Premenstrual Tension (*Syndrome*)
In the ten days or so before a menstrual period many women feel bloated, tense and irritable. In a few this may interfere with their concentration at work, their driving ability and their family life. The cause is hormonal. Vitamin B_6 helps about fifty per cent of

sufferers. For the rest, hormone treatments, usually consisting of taking progesterone, can be prescribed by your doctor.

Prolapse
The falling down or sinking of a part. It can occur with many organs including the back passage but is commonly used to describe 'sinking' of the womb into the vagina or bulging of the front and back walls of the vagina. The ligaments supporting the uterus and the tissues of the vagina may be inherently weak in some women and all are stretched during delivery of a baby. There are often no immediate symptoms in the young healthy mother but later, especially around the menopause when the tissues become less resilient, the symptoms of prolapse may appear. Symptoms include a feeling of 'something coming down' in the vaginal region. A swelling may be seen or there may be backache and vague lower abdominal discomfort. Difficulty in passing water, accidentally passing water while coughing or sneezing or recurrent cystitis (*see* CYSTITIS) may indicate that the front vaginal wall next to the bladder has dropped. Increasing constipation associated with a vaginal lump may mean that the back vaginal wall is bulging.

Careful attention to post natal exercises in the six weeks after childbirth may prevent the appearance of prolapse years later. These consist simply of tightening up the muscles which stop you passing water when you want to do so. This exercise can be performed twenty times a day as you are doing other jobs including washing up! The reward for doing the exercise may be also increased sex enjoyment. The same exercises may help to control mild prolapse when it first appears. Electrical treatment may also assist by stimulating the muscles. A ring pessary (*see* PESSARY) will control many cases of prolapse but needs regular changing (three to six months) by a doctor or nurse and young women would probably not wish to wear a pessary permanently. Operation to tighten up the ligaments and vaginal wall is probably best for most women. This is done from below so that there is no visible scar. After six to twelve weeks sex relations can be resumed and may even be improved by the tightening up of slack vaginal walls. Extra lubrication (e.g. KY jelly) may be needed at first and perhaps gentle dilatation by the woman's own fingers increasing gradually from one to three. Your gynaecologist will advise on the use of polythene dilators if this proves necessary but often simpler measures suffice.

If fibroids or some other condition is found to co-exist with a prolapse, the repair may be combined with a hysterectomy (*see* HYSTERECTOMY) also performed from below.

Prostate
A gland situated at the outlet of the bladder in men. Disease of the prostate interferes with the flow of urine.

Prostatitis
Inflammation of the gland can occur when germs enter from the urine. This condition causes fever, backache and trouble in passing water. It can also be a cause of general ill-health. Treatment is usually with antibiotics.

Prostate Cancer
A common but easily treated form of cancer which causes difficulty in passing water. The tumour can spread from the prostate into the bones. Treatment is by surgery and by the use of special hormone tablets or injections.

Benign Prostatic Hypertrophy
This is the commonest form of prostate trouble, a simple enlargement of the gland with increasing age.

If your water works are not functioning normally, or if you have pain passing water or discomfort in your bladder or sex organs, it may be something which will pass, but it could be an indication of an enlarged prostate.

If this happens act quickly, do not be shy; it is common, probably occurring in about twenty per cent of older men. Slight difficulty with the stream can progress to complete inability to empty the bladder, which would need insertion of a catheter (tube). Consult a doctor *immediately*, because a delay can cause *serious damage* and/or necessitate a major operation.

Treatment could require a prostatectomy; an easy operation today. Frequently it is performed through a tiny tube inserted into the urethra.

The operation involves the removal of part of the offending gland. This is often done by a wire being passed up the tube. The end of this is activated by an electric current which disintegrates the diseased parts.

The operation does not normally affect love-life or sex pleasure. For anatomical reasons the ejaculation of seminal fluid usually mostly or all passes into the bladder instead of as formerly. Consult with the surgeon to see if special treatment can be arranged to preserve fertility, and whether sex pleasures will be affected, then *accept his assurances*, because it is important to retain confidence. (*See* IMPOTENCE, FREQUENCY OF URINATION, RETENTION OF URINE.)

Pruritus
Medical term for itching. A particularly distressing form of intense pruritis known as pruritus vulvae (itching and inflammation of the external parts) occurs in women and is often due to thrush. This is common in diabetes (*see* DIABETES).

Psoriasis

A common skin disease in which hard, red, scaly patches appear. They often affect the skin near joints such as the elbows, or behind the knees, though other areas are often involved. Unfortunately the disease is a chronic one, and the patches are difficult to clear up. The exact cause is not known, but the disease is not dangerous. Sufferers often enjoy good health, although an associated arthritis may occur in some susceptible patients.

Treatment of psoriasis is a long-term problem. Local steroid, tar and dithranol ointments are often helpful. Recently a combination of tablets and special ultra-violet radiation (PUVA) has been found to help in many cases. Although the disease is nothing to do with cancer some anti-cancer drugs are also proving effective. Keep in touch with your doctor as advances may be on the way.

Psychosis

Describes any serious mental disturbance in which the patient has little or no insight into his condition. (*See* MENTAL ILLNESS.)

Pulse

The pulse is caused by an expansion of the arteries which corresponds with each heart beat. Counting the pulse is a convenient way of counting the heartbeats. In most infectious illnesses the heart beats faster than usual and the rate of the heartbeat often provides useful information to the doctor. A very slow pulse (forty beats a minute or less) if associated with other symptoms of ill health can indicate heart block or certain other serious illnesses. The treatment may be an artificial pacemaker (*see* HEART DISEASE). Athletes and many athletic people in robust health may have a slow pulse at rest (fifty beats or less a minute) and anyone with this tendency need not worry if their health is otherwise good. The pulse may be counted from any artery, but the one at the wrists is usually chosen. The radial artery runs over the bones at the front of the wrist below the base of the thumb. To count the pulse, the finger-tips should be placed in line over the artery with the patient's wrist straight, and the beats should be counted for a minute. (*See Fig. 10.*) The normal rate for an adult is about 70 to 80 beats per minute.

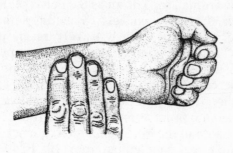

Fig 10. Taking the pulse

Purpura

A condition in which a rash of many small purplish red spots appears in the skin. There are several causes. It may be due to an abnormality of the blood in which the clotting mechanism has been interfered with, or to a disease of the smallest blood vessels, or capillaries, which allow a little blood to leak. The spots which are tiny collections of blood – about the size of a pinhead – may also form in the internal organs. Pressure on the spots causes them to pale as the blood is pushed to one side. The presence of purpura may indicate serious illness but in many cases the condition is merely a passing inconvenience as a mild type of purpura may sometimes accompany other infectious illness or may be a form of allergic response to a germ or drug.

Pus

When a part of the body is attacked by germs a thick fluid is often formed, known as *pus*. For further information *see* ABSCESS.

Pyelonephritis (*Pyelitis*)

The human kidney can be divided into two parts. The outer layer of the organ is made up of small blood vessels and tubes into which the impurities from the blood are filtered. These tubes open into an inner chamber or small sac known as the pelvis of the kidney, in which the urine collects. Sometimes this part is attacked by germs, which usually reach it via the bladder, and this condition is known as pyelitis. As there is always some degree of spread of infection from the collecting channels to the 'true' kidney the illness should really be thought of as pyelo*nephritis*. It is more common in women. (*See* CYSTITIS.) The symptoms are pain in the loin, pain and frequency in passing water and a very high temperature (105°F, 40½°C is not unusual). Sometimes there is vomiting and there may be attacks of shivering (rigors). The treatment of pyelonephritis is bed rest, plenty of fluids and appropriate antibiotics. Recurrent attacks indicate that more complete kidney investigation is called for and even one attack in a child needs specialist investigation.

Pyorrhoea

A chronic infection of the gums leading to discharge of pus and loosening of the teeth. It is not a condition which one can neglect. The sooner your dentist can start treatment the easier it should be to cure. The disease may possibly be prevented if the gums are brushed regularly up and down when cleaning the teeth. In old age, teeth may become loose through 'wear and tear'.

Pyrexia

(*See* FEVER *and* TEMPERATURE.)

Q

Quarantine (*and Incubation Periods*)
The period of time during which a disease may develop after exposure to infection. Most diseases have an incubation period, during which, although the germs are in the body, they do not produce symptoms. In a cold, for instance, the incubation period is usually three days – it takes three days to develop after 'catching' it from someone. During this period the illness is infectious although the carrier is still feeling well. Quarantine implies the shutting away of the suspect from all other contacts except necessary medical and nursing staff and immune people for a period of time equal to the incubation period plus two days. This is no longer necessary in the case of trivial or easily treated illnesses where more is lost than gained by the procedure. It is, however, vital in life-threatening illnesses like cholera, typhoid fever and poliomyelitis where all contacts should be strictly isolated during the quarantine period.

With the common childhood illnesses, the *sufferer* is of course excluded from school for certain periods which vary with the severity of the illness and local schools' requirements. You must be guided by your doctor. In dysentery and food poisoning the sufferer can return to work when medical testing of stool samples is found to be satisfactory. Those whose work is in any way connected with food should report to a doctor immediately with any symptoms such as nausea, vomiting, abdominal pain or loose motions.

Incubation periods for the common infections are shown:

Chicken pox	21 days	Measles	11 days
German measles	14–21 days	Mumps	14–21 days
Influenza	5 days	Whooping Cough	7–16 days

Quinsy

An abscess on the tonsil (*see* ABSCESS). The tonsil is liable to infection and sometimes this spreads beneath the tonsil where a small abscess forms. There is a fairly high temperature, considerable swelling of the throat, and pain. Penicillin is always necessary but sometimes the quinsy bursts releasing the pus. In severe cases it may have to be 'lanced' by the doctor.

R

Rabies (*See* DOG BITE.)

Rash

The name of an eruption on the skin. There are many types, all of which have special names:

Erythema is a diffuse redness of the skin – like a blush. It may follow exposure to the sun or a mild burn.

Macules are small patches on the skin which are *not* raised above the surface. A freckle could be described as a brown macule. Red macules occur in certain skin diseases.

Papules are small pimples on the skin. The rash of measles usually consists of a mixture of macules and papules. Thus there is a patchy discolouration of the skin, in some places *not* raised above the surface, and in other places raised into small bumps.

Vesicles are small blisters containing fluid. (They occur in chicken pox.)

Pustules are small blisters containing pus or 'matter'. They occur in ACNE and in many other conditions.

Raynaud's Disease

People develop white, numb fingers if subjected to intense cold. If they occur more readily and frequently than average it is known as Raynaud's phenomenon which means that the tiny arteries carrying blood to the fingers have clamped down to prevent blood entering the extremities. Sometimes it is a symptom of a more general disorder or it can be an isolated feature. The condition can be helped by tablets which open up blood vessels. (*See* CHILBLAIN, FROST BITE.)

221

Recovery Position

The recovery position should be used for the patient who is unconscious but *is* breathing. Putting someone in the recovery position will prevent the tongue from blocking the back of their airway (*see* ARTIFICIAL RESPIRATION) and ensure that they do not inhale their own vomit.

To place someone in the recovery position, you should kneel alongside the patient and tuck the arm nearest to you under his thigh. The arm must be straight and palm uppermost. Bring the other arm across the body and place the back of the patient's hand against his cheek.

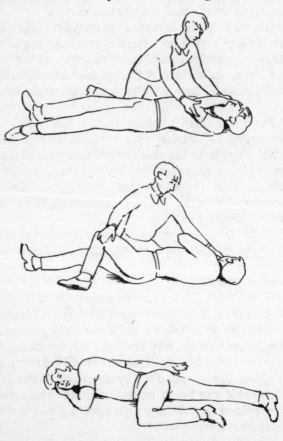

Hold it in this position with your hand. Use your other hand to bend the patient's further away leg so that his foot is alongside the nearer knee. Pull the patient towards you, using the bent knee as a handle. Ensure that your other hand continues to protect the patient's face. Pull the bent knee up into a right angle to his body to prevent him rolling on to his front. Adjust the lower arm to make sure he is not lying on it. Ensure that the airway is still clear and that the patient's face is resting on his own hand. Regularly recheck his breathing and call for an ambulance if this has not already been done.

Recuperation (*after an illness or operation*)
Some illnesses leave one weak and liable to a relapse.

After illness or operation, aim at recovering slowly, but *steadily*. That is the important point.

When in bed, and especially after surgery you will be advised to keep toes, legs, etc., moving. This is to prevent stagnation and thrombosis in a deep leg vein which could lead to a blood clot reaching the lung (*see* THROMBOSIS *and* EMBOLISM). Physical exercise strengthens, provided it is used wisely, regularly, and never beyond exhaustion point. The first day up one may manage only to walk ten yards, the next day fifty to one hundred yards may be possible. Do realise the speed at which returning physical and mental activity can surge back, even in the very old.

Avoid over-hot baths which can induce faintness. Healing tissues need plenty of vitamin C, obtainable from oranges or vitamin mixtures. Sunshine, too, is a great tonic (as well as promoting extra vitamin D in the skin) and a convalescent holiday in the sun is recommended. *It is the will to get well that matters.*

After even major operations, and illnesses such as coronary thrombosis, graduated walking exercises should get you ready for sedentary work by the six week stage. If you do manual work this may take longer: perhaps up to three months. You should also be ready to resume sexual intercourse somewhere between the six and twelve week stage. Talk to your doctor for specific advice.

After certain operations, especially abdominal ones, coughing can cause hernias so smokers are advised to give it up. Straining to open the bowels can have the same effect.

Healing of long bones may require prolonged immobilisation in hospital. Here the importance of the will to get well is even more vital. Full cooperation with prescribed exercises and physiotherapy is usually the mainstay of treatment – active exercise often being more important than passive massage, etc.

Renal Colic
It sometimes happens that stones form within the kidney – usually in the collecting part of the kidney, or pelvis (*see* PYELONEPHRITIS). If the stone is small it may try to pass from the kidney to the bladder through a narrow tube known as the ureter. This usually causes a severe pain which comes on in spasms and is known as *renal colic*. This pain commonly starts in the loin and radiates downwards towards the groin on the same side. It may be accompanied by blood in the urine due to injury to the ureter as the stone passes through it. The condition calls for expert investigation and treatment, usually in hospital where X-rays and other means of investigation are available. The presence of blood in the water (Haematuria) is always an indication of something amiss and should demand medical attention. (*See* CALCULUS, KIDNEY DISEASES, PROSTATE.)

Retention of Urine
When urine has collected in the bladder the pressure rises and we feel a desire to pass water. When circumstances permit, we allow the muscle guarding the exit from the bladder to relax and it is emptied. *Retention of urine* means that there is some interference with this emptying and either the bladder cannot be emptied (*acute reten-*

tion) or emptying is not complete. Acute retention most often occurs in elderly men due to a swelling of the prostate gland. Medical assistance must be sent for at once, and it is often essential for the doctor to pass a tube (catheter) to draw off the urine. Acute retention can occur in women during the early months of pregnancy, when, if the womb becomes displaced, it may press on the lower part of the bladder. It is usually not difficult to 'replace' the womb when the condition clears. Difficulty in passing water usually precedes retention. Seek advice now and do not wait until it is serious. (*See* PREGNANCY, PROSTATE.)

Sometimes inability to pass urine is due to shyness, for example, in a public toilet or hospital. This has no physical cause and cures in time. Certain drugs can also cause this.

Retina

The innermost of the three coats surrounding the eye; it is the part sensitive to light and which registers images.

Sometimes it becomes displaced and may lead to blindness unless treated urgently by laser.

Retinitis Pigmentosa

A hereditary condition in which the retina becomes progressively thickened and coated with pigment (coloured material) so that vision gradually deteriorates. Research into methods of treatment continues.

Retroversion

The tipping of an entire organ backward. The term is commonly used to describe the womb (uterus). Twenty per cent of women are born with the uterus lying in this position and unless it is giving rise to discomfort or contributing to infertility no treatment is needed.

Reye's Syndrome

A rare but serious illness in children, usually when recovering from influenza or chicken pox. The child becomes drowsy and may lapse into coma. The cause is unknown but it is more likely to occur if aspirin has been given. For this reason, aspirin should not be used in children unless prescribed for arthritis.

Rhesus Factor
As well as being classified into A, O, B and AB groups, blood can be divided into *rhesus positive* and *rhesus negative* types depending on the presence or absence of rhesus factors in the red blood cells. Problems used to arise when a rhesus negative mother married to a rhesus positive father gave birth to a rhesus positive baby. The mother manufactured 'antibodies' to the baby's red blood cells which had crossed into her circulation through the placenta (*see* BIRTH). These antibodies could then pass back into the baby's blood through the umbilical cord and destroy his red blood cells causing jaundice and anaemia.

The danger period for the passage of baby red cells into the maternal blood is at the time of a birth or miscarriage when the placenta separates from the uterus lining. This explains why a first baby was usually unaffected (unless there had been a previous miscarriage).

A great advance in recent years has been the introduction of 'Anti-Rhesus D' serum which is now given to rhesus negative mothers in the UK at the time of each delivery or miscarriage. This serum 'mops up' any baby red cells which have got into the mother's circulation before they have had time to induce antibodies. There has thus been a great reduction in numbers of severely affected babies needing exchange blood transfusion or being damaged by jaundice.

In the UK mothers are routinely blood grouped and tested for antibodies at various stages of pregnancy so that 'at risk' babies can be detected before birth and perhaps induced early if this seems to be in their best interests. Due to 'Anti D' these premature inductions are becoming rarer.

Rheumatic Fever

Now a rare illness in the UK but still common in Asia, it usually follows a throat infection with a particular type of streptococcus germ. After an interval of about six weeks the body's fighting forces including antibodies over-react and turn on its own tissues, particularly the joints, and cause inflammation. These reactions may also involve the muscle and valves of the heart. A fever, sore throat and swollen painful joints are typical.

Occasionally the brain may become involved leading to the jerky, uncontrolled movements known as St Vitus' Dance (see CHOREA). Antibiotics, especially penicillin, are effective in curing the original streptococcal infection and help to prevent Rheumatic Fever nowadays. Reasons for its rarity are changes in the nature of the streptococcus which has become a milder germ and the improved health of children. If it *does* develop, treatment is bedrest to rest the joints and the heart and a prolonged course of penicillin. Sometimes after recovery, which may take several weeks, the patient is left with a damaged heart valve. Modern surgical techniques are often effective in repairing or replacing the valves.

Rheumatism

A vague term covering conditions associated with pain in the joints or limbs. Rheumatism which affects the joints is more accurately known as ARTHRITIS, and the reader should consult this article. Other varieties of the condition are described under MUSCULAR RHEUMATISM and BACKACHE.

Rheumatoid Arthritis (*See* ARTHRITIS.)

Rickets

A deficiency disease, due to lack of vitamin D which affects growing children. For the proper growth and strengthening of bones calcium is required, and it cannot be absorbed from the diet and utilized by the body without the aid of small quantities of vitamin D. This vitamin occurs chiefly in milk and butter, but can also be manufactured by the body with the aid of sunlight – but not without. If the diet is lacking in the vitamin-containing foods, and if the child does not receive much sunshine, then the absorption of calcium is liable to fall below the minimum requirements. When this happens growth is stunted and the bones become soft and bend. *Rickets* is rare in England because steps are taken to see that all children have adequate vitamin D. Flour, margarine and cereals usually have vitamin D added artificially and vitamin drops are provided at welfare clinics for the under fives. However, the disease is still seen in Asian children in the UK and in many parts of the world where poverty and malnutrition exist.

Rigor

An attack of shivering which occurs when the temperature is raised. When the body wishes to increase its temperature one of the ways it can do this is by shivering. This sets the muscles working in little to and fro movements, which generate heat. Normally, when the body becomes chilled shivering is liable to occur. If the body is invaded by germs and the temperature rises suddenly, severe shivering attacks may occur and these are known as *rigors*. Nature at work! (*See* PYELONEPHRITIS *and* MALARIA.)

Ringworm

Caused by a fungus, or yeast-like organism, which attacks the skin and the roots of the hairs. It is contagious and may occur in epidemics, for instance in schools. It commonly affects the hairy skin at the back of the neck, and the infection spreads in a circular fashion, forming a round area which gives the disease its name. Tablets and creams from the doctor will cure the condition.

Rubella (*See* GERMAN MEASLES.)

S

Salmonella

A common cause of outbreaks of gastro-enteritis when diarrhoea and vomiting occur over several days. It is a germ similar to typhoid and is due to eating contaminated food (*see* FOOD POISONING) or drinking water which has not been treated. It is most serious in children or the elderly.

Salpingitis

The top of the womb is connected by means of two small tubes, the Fallopian tubes, to the ovaries, one on either side of the lower part of the abdominal cavity. When the tubes become inflamed the condition is known as *salpingitis,* which may accompany or follow any infection of the womb and vagina. One cause is neglected gonorrhoea, in which the infection gradually works its way up until the tubes are involved. Less common nowadays is tuberculous salpingitis. Salpingitis, in common with most infections, is usually accompanied by fever, and there is pain low down on either side of the abdomen. (If the right tube is affected, the condition may be mistaken for appendicitis.) A common cause is infection with an organism called chlamydia. Salpingitis must be not neglected, as it frequently causes sterility. Treatment is by antibiotics and radiant heat. (*See* ECTOPIC PREGNANCY, GONORRHOEA *and* INFERTILITY.)

Sarcoidosis

A disorder which may affect many organs including the skin, glands, lungs and liver. The first signs are often purple patches on the shins known as erythema nodosum. If the lungs are involved there may be shortness of breath. Fortunately the condition responds well to steroids so unusual patches on the shins should always be mentioned to your doctor in case these are an early sign (although there are other more trivial causes).

Scabies

A skin disease known as the 'itch' and caused by a small mite. It makes small burrows in the skin where it lays its eggs; and since it is active when the skin is warm, the itching is usually at its worst in bed at night, or when sitting by the fire. The hands, particularly the webs of the fingers, and the wrists are the parts most often affected. It is contagious, being passed from one to another, and like louse infestation is favoured by overcrowding and lack of cleanliness.

Treatment consists in having a hot bath and scrubbing the affected parts with a stiff brush to open up the burrows, changing and boiling all the clothing and bedclothes, and applying something to kill the mites. One of the most effective is Benzyl Benzoate or Quellada lotion applied to the whole body from neck downwards and left for 24 hours before washing off. Two applications separated by five days nearly always cure but unless the clothes are properly dealt with, and all the members of the family are cleared, re-infection is likely.

Scalds
(*See* BURNS.)

Scarlet Fever (*Scarlatina*)

Once a killing disease scarlet fever is less serious because the germ which causes it, a streptococcus, has become less violent. It is infectious with a short incubation period (3–5 days) starting as a sore throat, tonsillitis and fever. A skin rash appears a day or two later with a general reddening (erythema) except around the mouth area which is pale. It responds rapidly to penicillin and long-term complications such as acute nephritis and rheumatic fever are now rare.

Schizophrenia
Describes a seriously disordered mind, where thought and behaviour lose touch with reality, i.e. in the acute stage the sufferer is psychotic. There are several types, including the paranoid form, and sufferers may be suspicious, possibly only of some people. In the classical form, thinking becomes disjointed and the emotions and reactions inappropriate. The patient may hear 'voices' giving instructions, and because of this may occasionally act dangerously. Judgment and control of emotions suffer, delusions are common, and the person can become unwilling or unable to cooperate with friends and medical advisers. He may end in collapse. The invalid is unbalanced, and his family 'do not know what to do'.

The interaction of mind on body is poorly understood. Nevertheless, counselling, psychotherapy and consideration of change in the life-style are likely to be of help, but only after the acute stage of this illness is controlled. In the early days the sufferer needs urgent medical help which may include long-term medication and occasionally ECT. (*See* ANXIETY STATE, DEPRESSION, ELECTRO CONVULSIVE THERAPY, MENTAL ILLNESS, PARANOIA.)

Sciatica
Term for pain in the sciatic nerve, a large nerve running through the buttock and down the back of the leg. It occurs when the nerve becomes inflamed due to pressure from a slipped (or prolapsed) disc (*see* SLIPPED DISC), on its origins in the lumbar region. The bones of the spine or vertebrae are separated by a small disc of 'gristle', and if one of these intervertebral discs becomes displaced it may press upon an adjacent nerve root. Sciatica can be very painful but will often respond

231

to simple remedies such as rest and tablets to reduce inflammation but, if this fails, traction and occasionally an operation may be required. Sometimes an injection into the disc by a specialist may be given in the acute stage to relieve the pain. See your doctor.

Scurvy
Deficiency disease, due to lack of vitamin C. Vitamin C is necessary to keep the blood vessels healthy, and in its absence the small capillaries become weak and allow bleeding into the skin and gums, as well as lowered resistance to infections. Vitamin C is found in fresh fruits and vegetables, of which nearly everyone can have an adequate supply. The disease is practically unknown in the UK, but occasionally occurs in the poor, the elderly or in those who adopt a peculiar diet which does not include fruit or vegetables. However, it is common in Third World countries during famine.

Sea Sickness
(*See* TRAVEL SICKNESS *and* VOMITING.)

Sebaceous Cyst
(*See* CYST.)

Second Opinion
The term means a second consultant opinion but most people use it to mean any specialist opinion arranged by the family doctor.

Your family doctor will have many consultant colleagues and access to a variety of specialist departments. Often he will suggest that you see a consultant if he feels it necessary. If he does not, it may be because he is confident about the nature of your condition thinking you will obtain no benefit from further investigation or surgery. Occasionally it may be because you have minimised your symptoms or anxieties and implied that you feel better than you do.

If you are anxious about some symptoms tell him just how worried you are and why (e.g. a family history of some illness). Often a relation can put this over better than you and a word from one is often useful. Once they understand the reason for anxiety most doctors will arrange a consultant appointment. If this fails, put your request in writing. Some people are better at expressing themselves in this way and few doctors will refuse a written request. Although a specialist will sometimes see you privately without a letter of reference from your doctor he will often prefer you to have one. However, there is usually a way round any difficulty. It should rarely be necessary to change doctors but this is possible in extreme cases.

Septicaemia

Implies that germs are multiplying fast in the blood and have almost overcome body defences. Fever then delirium occur and urgent appropriate antibiotic treatment is needed.

Sexually Transmitted Diseases (STD)

HIV INFECTION (AIDS), SYPHILIS and GONORRHOEA apart, the most common is non-specific urethritis (*see* NSU) often due to a germ, Chlamydia. Despite treatment, complications can occur in eyes, and joints. TRICHOMONAS and THRUSH which give vaginal discharge can spread by intercourse as can a grave form of HEPATITIS. Pubic LICE are also spread by intercourse. *There are more risks to casual sex than is supposed.*

The *herpes virus* (HSV-2) is another cause of STD. Genital herpes usually causes sore blisters of the genitalia in both sexes. It is increasing, probably due to permissive attitudes and more use of *non-barrier* birth control. It can be recurrent and may affect the health of an unborn child if an attack occurs in pregnancy. It may be implicated in the development of cancer of the cervix some years afterwards. Until recently there was

233

no satisfactory treatment but a new anti-viral drug 'Acyclovir' seems effective.

Shaking
(*See* TREMOR.)

Shingles
A virus infection the same as in CHICKEN POX. In shingles, damage is confined to an area supplied to a nerve. The common site is the trunk, but it may affect the face or limbs. Usually burning pain is felt before other symptoms, followed by eruption. Small patches of skin are inflamed, on each are small spots with white tops on a strip of skin supplied by one nerve. In the trunk they follow a circle from back to front. Usually it lasts a few weeks, thcn subsides. Normally recovery is complete in about three to four weeks; but sometimes, particularly in the elderly, there is some persistent pain after the eruption has gone. Soothing lotions such as calamine can be helpful and an anti-virus agent (available only on prescription) if started early may reduce the severity of the pain and inflammation. This should always be given if the eye is being affected. Elderly people sometimes are helped by special pain-killing tablets for persistent post-shingles pain. Susceptible subjects can catch chicken pox from people with shingles.

Shock
Medically this term means collapse of the circulation, when the blood pressure is low and the flow of blood through the tissues is reduced. It occurs most commonly after blood loss or with severe pain. The pulse becomes fast and weak, the skin pale and clammy and the breathing shallow or laboured. It requires urgent medical attention. If the patient is injured do not move him; keep him calm, ensure that breathing is unrestricted by tight clothes and keep him warmly wrapped

in a blanket until medical help arrives.

Sickle Cell Disease (Anaemia)
A hereditary form of chronic anaemia in which haemo-
lytic crises occur (in which the red blood cells self-
destruct). It is found in the eastern Mediterranean,
Africa and Asia. It is inherited by passing the gene
from affected parent to the child and the disease
occurs when the dominant gene appears.

The disease is always associated with chronic
anaemia, ill health and bone pain.

Unfortunately it has a very high mortality rate and
until bone marrow transplantation was made available
for a few cases no specific treatment was available.

Sickness
(*See* TRAVEL SICKNESS *and* VOMITING.)

Sinus
A hollow cavity often taken to mean one of the hollows
in the facial bones communicating with the nose. (*See*
ANTRUM.) But also a term used for a discharging hole
anywhere in the body, commonly seen after operations
when a hidden stitch or foreign body may be the cause.

Sinusitis
(*See* ANTRUM.)

Sleep
(*See* page 13 *and* INSOMNIA.)

Slipped Disc (*Prolapsed Disc*)
The spine consists of a column of strong bones
(vertebrae) separated by tough but compressible
'discs'. Occasionally a disc, which is rather like a
cushion, becomes damaged or swollen and its gelatinous 'stuffing' is squeezed out by the pressure from the
vertebrae. This causes pressure on surrounding tissues

(prolapse) and the result is severe back pain. When the nerves emerging from the spinal cord are compressed by the disc material the result is sciatica, pain in the buttock and leg. Tingling or numbness in the calf or foot often follows. A slipped disc can be treated in many ways. Bed rest, a supporting plaster or corset, and traction (to pull the vertebrae steadily off the protruding disc) are often used, as are injections into the disc. Relief of pain is probably due to shrivelling up of the extruded matter rather than its returning back to the disc shell.

Back strengthening exercises (*see* BACKACHE) are useful after the pain has subsided. The value of a plaster or surgical corset is that the spine can be rested while the patient continues to be up and about. Although uncomfortable this is usually preferable to a long time in bed. Occasionally, severe cases benefit from an operation in which the damaged disc is removed (laminectomy).

As the disc nucleus is made of soft gelatinous material it is unlikely in most cases that it can be 'put back'. More likely, manipulation stretches and tears a few pieces of fibrous tissue allowing the disc to settle down into a more comfortable area with less pressure on a nerve. Everyone should aim to put as little cruel stress on the vertebral column as possible by always bending the knees to pick any item off the floor. The majority of slipped discs respond to the conservative measures outlined above plus common sense in everyday life.

Not every acute backache is due to a slipped disc. There are probably all sorts of minor displacements between the many facets of vertebrae which cause pain. There is every degree of back problem ranging from the minor nuisance variety to the completely paralysing when the muscle of the thigh wastes away due to longstanding or recurrent sciatica. Low back pain problems are often due to poor posture and lack of care in the workplace and are the commonest causes of industrial sickness.

Smallpox
Has now been eradicated worldwide.

Snakebite
Unless hospital treatment by anti-venom cannot be obtained fairly quickly it is better to do nothing except allay anxiety. Get the patient to hospital as soon as possible, and take the killed snake along for identification. If a very long delay is anticipated a broad, flat firm compress may be applied but on no account should a narrow, constricting band be used as its release may cause sudden flooding of the system with poison.

Spina Bifida
A defect in the closure of the bony cages of the spinal cord at the time of its development before birth. Thus there may be protrusion of nervous tissue or its covering usually at a low level on the baby's back. In the least affected cases the skin is intact, only the bony cage being defective; in such types there may be no nerve damage and the condition may simply be noted by chance on X-ray.

Where there is considerable exposure of nervous tissue the patient has paralysis and loss of sensation in the pelvis and legs, including loss of control of bladder and bowel. In milder cases there is a variable degree of weakness and sensation loss.

Where possible the defect is closed surgically soon after birth but such children need intensive orthopaedic and neurological supervision to make the best use of existing faculties and to prevent muscles from contracting into a fixed, bent position. Closure of the gap may predispose to the build up of fluid circulating through the spinal canal and can cause hydrocephalus (enlargement of the head due to increased fluid in the cerebral canal) but this problem has been largely overcome by the development of a one way valve inserted near the ear to connect the brain cavity with the blood circulation. Mothers who have had one such baby or where there is a family history of the condition can have a test performed on the womb fluid at the sixteenth week of any subsequent pregnancy. The presence of a certain protein in the fluid indicates the likelihood that the baby does have a spinal defect and the mother is offered termination of pregnancy if she wishes.

There is now medical evidence that this condition may be associated with vitamin and mineral deficiency during conception and/or early pregnancy. For this reason, such women should be given vitamin and mineral supplements before they become pregnant.

Spleen
The spleen lies in the upper part of the abdominal cavity on the left, under the lowest ribs. It stores blood corpuscles and releases these into the circulation if they are required in an emergency. It also removes the old, worn-out blood cells from circulation. The spleen, if badly injured, can be removed without any apparent ill effects. But people who have undergone a splenectomy should carry a card with that information and inform doctors of this when seeking any medical advice.

Sprains
Joints are held together by tough bands of tissue known as ligaments. If a joint is carried beyond its normal range of movement, by a sudden twist, for instance, the ligaments binding it may be strained or torn. This is known as a *sprain*. There is pain in the joint which persists, and soon the joint becomes swollen and stiff. One of the common joints to be sprained is the ankle, which is usually turned under while walking or running on a rough surface. The best initial treatment is a cold compress which helps to reduce the swelling. Rest for a

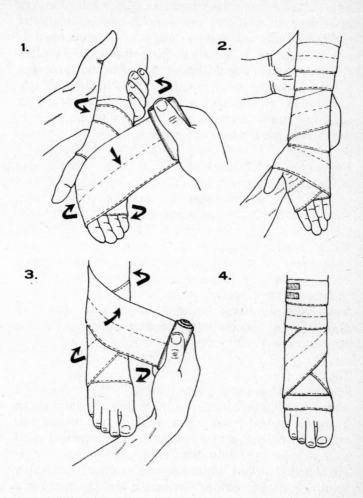

Fig. 11 Bandaging a sprain

day or two is usually needed but activity can then be resumed, provided that the joint has support. An elastic bandage or arthro-pad is useful; the former should be applied in a figure of eight around the foot and lower end of the leg *(see Fig. 11)*. It should be worn until the tenderness and swelling have gone, in possibly a few days to a fortnight. The wrist too is often sprained, and it should be supported in the same way with a spiral bandage applied from the knuckles to about half way to the elbow. Consult a doctor for serious sprains, for there may be injury to the bone, in addition to the ligament injury.

Sprue (*Coeliac Disease*)

Occurs when absorption of food from the intestines is interfered with for some reason. The patient loses weight, may become anaemic and has loose motions which have a fatty appearance. The usual cause in the UK is Coeliac Disease in which sensitivity to gluten (a constituent of wheatgerm) can damage the delicate intestinal lining. A gluten-free diet restores normality.

Tropical sprue occurs when some form of infection leaves the intestinal lining damaged and unable to absorb food adequately. Medical investigation is required in a specialist centre.

Sputum

Matter which is coughed up. Normally there should be none, for although there is a slight secretion within the bronchi, or breathing tubes, it does not collect sufficiently to come up on coughing. The production of sputum is an indication that the bronchi are irritated. It often occurs in heavy smokers who inhale – when the sputum is dark in colour. Sputum is also produced in a number of diseases. Bronchitis, pneumonia and tuberculosis are examples. Any persistent cough (three weeks or more) with which sputum is produced should be taken as a warning that a medical overhaul is advisable.

Squint

Normally the eyes are co-ordinated so they point in the same direction. This enables the brain to make one picture from the images received from the separate eyes. When there is a squint (strabismus) the eye muscles are out of balance so that one eye points inwards or outwards. This makes it difficult for the brain to fuse the two images, so that after a time the affected eye becomes 'lazy' and takes little part in vision. It is important that a squint should be treated early before the affected eye has grown lazy. Squinting is only normal in the first few weeks of life and if neglected the eye will eventually become sightless. If it persists after three months seek advice. Treatment may be by a combination of exercises, covering the sound eye for a time in order to make the squinting eye do more work, by prescribing glasses, and sometimes operation to improve the cosmetic effect.

St Vitus' Dance

(*See* CHOREA.)

Stammering

Speech defect in which there is a recurrent hesitation in the flow of words. There are different types of stammering, one of the most common being a repetition of the beginning of a word, especially if it begins with a consonant (e.g. c-c-c-c-consonant). The condition is always made worse by nervousness, which often sets up a vicious circle, the patient being afraid that he will stammer and therefore stammering more. Seek expert treatment for a young child who stammers. Special methods of speech-therapy have been developed, and it is easier to cure the abnormality before it is firmly established. Ask your local Child Clinic (in the UK) if you are anxious in any way about your four-year-old child's speech. Hearing may need to be checked and if speech therapy does prove to be necessary this will allow plenty of time before starting school. Although many minor defects at this stage are simply due to immaturity it is better to be certain about hearing acuity and speech.

Stings
Insects, bees, wasps and ants, etc., are able to injure tissues by injecting material by means of a special sting or biting. The material which produces the irritation is usually an acid, and the pain can sometimes be alleviated by applying an alkali. This may be done by using a wet compression on which sodium bicarbonate has been sprinkled. One exception is the wasp which produces an alkaline sting so that an application of vinegar may be soothing. Stings are usually not serious, but scratching should be avoided since it may introduce germs and so lead to infection. Be wary to watch every bite when out picnicking. Wasp stings on the tongue can be dangerous leading to swelling which can cause breathing difficulties. Urgent medical attention is necessary.

It is possible to become allergic to insect stings and if your skin reaction seems to be excessive, consult your doctor so as to avoid future trouble. In extreme allergic reactions there may be swelling of the throat causing breathing difficulties and collapse of the circulation. You should have antihistamine tablets with you if you are allergic to bee stings, but probably the best emergency treatment for allergy to bee stings is the use of an adrenaline inhaler. This inhaler was originally designed as an asthma treatment but is quicker and more effective than the injections previously recommended for severe sting allergy. In the UK ask your doctor about this as a prescription is needed.

Insect repellant creams which are not unpleasant to use can be purchased at all chemists' shops and these may reduce insect attacks.

Stones

(*See* CALCULUS, RENAL COLIC *and* GALL BLADDER.)

Stroke

Broadly speaking, the right half of the body is controlled by the left half of the brain and vice versa. A stroke often causes a weakness of one half of the body. It is due to damage to the opposite half of the brain, and nearly always results from some interference with the blood supply. One of the causes is a *cerebral* haemorrhage in which there is bleeding into the tissues of the brain due to a rupture of a blood vessel. This is sometimes a late consequence of untreated high blood pressure, or it may be due to a weak patch in one of the arteries in the brain. In other cases the stroke is not due to bleeding but to a blood clot in one of the arteries, which deprives a part of the brain of its blood. Sometimes the clot forms in the vessel due perhaps to a rough patch on the wall. This is a *cerebral thrombosis.* Or the clot may form elsewhere and be carried to the brain in the circulation, plugging one of the arteries – a *cerebral embolism.*

Whatever the cause the results are similar. The patient may become unconscious, one half of the body may be found to be weakened and there may be loss of speech.

Recovery is often complete, perhaps within a week or two. Often much smaller strokes occur in which there may be only slight weakness of one limb or slurring of speech and recovery may take place within an hour or two (TIA – Temporary Ischaemic Attack).

These very small strokes are often referred to as 'spasms', the assumption being that a blood vessel has closed up – then opened again. 'Spasms' are a useful warning as they often allow some risk factors such as high blood pressure to be recognised and treated.

Even with larger strokes there is often a considerable recovery, since the remaining undamaged parts of the brain are able to take over many of the functions of the damaged part. This takes time and calls for perseverance by the patient. Usually the younger the victim the more the recovery that can be expected, and anyone who has suffered from a stroke must never give up hope.

Physiotherapy can be arranged and if exercises are carried out regularly, slow but steady improvement will usually reward the victim. A useful exercise for a weak hand is to squeeze a soft ball (or plastic pan scourer) twenty times four times a day. Speech therapy is helpful for those whose speech is affected and this may also include retraining in handwriting. The local Social Service Departments (in the UK) are very helpful in suggesting and fitting devices in the home to make daily living easier for a stroke victim. Your family doctor can put you in touch with the various agencies who are able to help.

It has been shown that the majority of strokes are related to raised (or high) blood pressure. For this reason everyone over 50 (and certainly over 60) should have their blood pressure measured. Many chemists now offer this service and all doctors.

Stye
A small boil which develops on the eyelid due to infection at the root of one of the eyelashes. It usually clears spontaneously but may be helped by using an antiseptic eye ointment. Recurrent styes may indicate the need for an antibiotic eye ointment and medical investigation into general health.

Suffocation
Occurs when the body is deprived of air for some reason. (*See* ASPHYXIA *and* ARTIFICIAL RESPIRATION.)

Sulphonamides
These drugs were discovered originally during research

into chemical dyes; they combat bacterial infections in a similar way to antibiotics. Sulphonamides have been largely superseded by ANTIBIOTICS but are still used in the treatment of bowel disorders such as ulcerative colitis and Crohn's disease.

Sunburn

After exposure to sun the skin produces a brown pigment which helps to protect it from damage by ultra-violet rays. The development of a 'tan' takes time, and if the skin is exposed for too long before this has occurred, it may be severely burnt. *The symptoms are delayed*, so the fact one feels comfortable while sunbathing is no guarantee that damage is not being done. People vary in their sensitivity, fair and redheads usually being more sensitive than people with dark hair. Take special care when coming into contact with strong sunlight for the first time after winter. Half an hour sunbathing is probably more than enough on the first day and this may be increased daily if there is no soreness. If the skin has become burnt, all exposure must be stopped until the burn subsides. Protective suntan creams should be applied before sunbathing. The higher the factor, the greater the protection afforded. For those who cannot tolerate sunlight at all, preparations such as Uvistat or Spectraban are helpful; these latter are almost totally impervious to sunlight. Remember also that the time spent bathing must be counted in the time of exposure since ultra-violet rays penetrate some distance in water. If you do get burned a useful cream, which can be obtained from the chemist, is caladryl; but this must be kept out of the eyes and mouth. Over exposure to the sun can lead to skin cancer later.

Sunstroke

Due to over-exposure to the sun especially of head and neck, and caused by overheating. Sunlight is rich in infra-red rays which cause heating of the body tissues. Prolonged exposure without any head and neck covering is liable to be followed by severe headache and general prostration. Prevention is easy. No one should remain long in strong sun without adequate cover, preferably of light colour which must also shade the back of the neck. The headache which results in the unwary can usually be relieved by soluble aspirin or Paracetamol, and for severe cases a day in bed following the exposure will usually cure. In hot climates, extra salt is required with food in order to replace that lost by excessive sweating.

Suppuration (*Festering*)
(*See* ABSCESS.)

Syphilis
After AIDS, the most serious of the sexually transmitted diseases – i.e. diseases spread by sexual contact, due to a specific germ, a spirochaete. The disease can be divided into well-marked stages. The incubation period is usually four to five weeks but may vary between 10 and 90 days. The first symptom (primary stage) is a small painless spot at the site of infection, usually the genitals, but very occasionally elsewhere such as the lips. This spot breaks down into an ulcer or small sore, oozing serum which is highly infective; and the glands in the neighbourhood often become a little swollen. The severity of this sore, or *chancre*, is variable; and it may be small and only temporary. It is liable to be missed especially in women because of its internal situation. Because of this, any young person who has indulged in casual sex relations should be checked in a VD (special) clinic even if there are vague symptoms or no symptoms at all. The use of barrier methods of contraception such as cap or sheath give some protection against syphilis but the contraceptive pill gives no protection. In a totally steady sexual

relationship where each partner is faithful to the other and each has no history of infection there is, of course, no risk of venereal disease. Where sex is taken casually there is always danger of infection and if worried it is wise to put your mind at rest by clinic checks. It is also a good idea to make sure that the man always uses a sheath.

Lists of special clinics in the UK can be found in the telephone directory and all treatment and advice is secret. As the long-term effects of syphilis are so dangerous it is vital that sexual contacts are traced and clinic staff help in this task. Patients are obviously told to refrain from sexual relations until treatment is completed. Occasionally patients will not comply with this but at least they can make sure that a sheath is worn.

From the site of infection the spirochaete passes into the blood and is distributed thoughout the body. This is the secondary stage. Usually there is a generalised rash which develops three or four weeks after the chancre, and the glands in other parts of the body may enlarge. The rash takes different forms, and may be associated with ulcers in the mouth and some falling of the hair. From the second stage the disease passes into the third, in which deep, painless ulcers, known as gummata, may form in various internal organs and skin. In the late stages the nervous system is particularly liable to be attacked. There may be a slow paralysis in which walking becomes more and more unsteady due to degeneration of the spinal cord known as *tabes dorsalis*; or in other cases the brain is affected, and there is a generalised paralysis together with progressive mental impairment – a condition known as *general paralysis of the insane* (GPI). Practically no organ in the body is immune in the late stages of untreated syphilis. The heart may be damaged, the liver affected and vision lost. The course of the disease is slow, and symptoms involving the nervous system may develop twenty or

247

more years after the original infection. The disease is practically never caught apart from sexual union, since the spirochaete dies rapidly outside the human body; infection from a lavatory seat is very unlikely. Infection through kissing is rare, although chancres on the lip can be contracted by orogenital sexual acts. Syphilis can be passed to the unborn child of an infected mother but this condition is now rare. All pregnant women in the UK are tested for the disease at their first antenatal hospital appointment.

Syphilis can be cured. Early treatment is essential. It cannot be too strongly emphasised that the disease is insidious, and any suspicious symptoms in anyone who has run a danger of infection should lead to advice being sought. It is dangerous and extremely foolish to stop treatment before your doctor is satisfied that it has been sufficient.

There is no real prevention against syphilis except the avoidance of casual sex; the promiscuous will always run into danger of infection.

T

Tachycardia

Term for an increased heart rate. This commonly occurs when the temperature is raised (*see* PULSE); or with a normal temperature may be due to nervousness when it is associated with palpitations. It is occasionally due to heart disease, and another not uncommon cause is an overaction of the thyroid gland. (*See* GOITRE, PALPITATIONS.)

Talipes *(Clubfoot)*

A deformity of the foot, present at birth, in which the foot is twisted and fixed inwards or out. The more serious is known as equinovarus where the heel is turned inwards from the midline of the leg and the foot is bent under. In mild cases, massage and splinting may suffice to straighten the foot. For serious types, operation is needed to divide the ligaments which are holding the foot abnormally. Due to careful orthopaedic surgery, most of these youngsters end up with near-perfect feet and the ugly old condition of clubfoot is disappearing.

Temperature

Temperature – How to take it

1. Hold the thermometer between the finger and thumb at the top end, away from the bulb.
2. Stand facing the light and hold the thermometer horizontally a little below the eyes. Find the markings

249

and figures which show the level of the temperature.

3. Roll the thermometer slightly backwards and forwards between finger and thumb. The light will be reflected from the mercury in the small central tube.

Fig. 12   The thermometer
Showing both Fahrenheit and Centigrade

4. If the mercury is up in the stem of the thermometer shake it down into the bulb with a few vigorous jerks.

5. Look again and make quite sure that the mercury is down. Place the thermometer bulb well inside the mouth beneath the tongue, or, in the case of a child, in the armpit while holding the arm to the side.

6. Leave the thermometer in the mouth for at least a full minute, or beneath the arm for two minutes.

7. Hold the thermometer to the light again, turn it to reflect the mercury and find the level as described above (3).

8. Compare the mercury with the readings. The degrees are marked by numbers – 97°. 102°, etc., Fahrenheit or 37°, 38°, etc., Centigrade, known also as Celsius. Some thermometers show dual scales. Between each number are marked ten small divisions. Find the number next below the mercury level and then count up the small divisions until the level is reached. This gives the temperature. Thus if the mercury is three divisions above 99° the temperature is 99.3 (ninety-nine point three). In most thermometers the normal temperature level (98.4) is marked by a small arrow, while in Centigrade normal is approximately 37°. After using the thermometer, do *not* wash in hot water as it will burst.

Tennis Elbow

Caused by strain of the muscles which straighten the arm at the elbow. Rarely caused by tennis, it often follows activities like house painting where the strain is more sustained. The arm needs rest for up to three weeks. An arthro-pad worn for a day or two will often speed recovery. One or two injections of hydrocortisone and local anaesthetic into the tender spots, if required, will usually cure. The pain may feel worse for 24 hours after the injection before improving. Heat and manipulation may be useful in stubborn cases, or a small operation.

Tenosynovitis

The tendons or leaders at the back of the hand and arm which move the fingers and wrist are encased in sheaths. The inner parts of these sheaths can become inflamed due to over-strain, causing pain and a cracking sound on movement. The condition is common in young adults where work demands excessive movement of the wrist and hand. It is also common in gardeners. The wrist should be immobilized in plaster or a plaster bandage for three weeks and excessive use of the fingers and thumb avoided for two months. In recurrent cases injection with hydro-cortisone or even an operation may be needed (see your doctor).

Test Tube Baby
(*See* INFERTILITY.)

Testicle
(*See* ORCHITIS, UNDESCENDED TESTICLE, VARICOCELE).

Tetanus (*See also* IMMUNISATION.)

This disease, known as lock jaw, is due to a specific germ. The poison from the tetanus bacillus has an action on the cells of the nervous system – which send the messages to move muscles. It causes irritability in these cells which results in a spasm, or painful contraction of the muscles. The jaw muscles may be involved, hence the name. The germ may gain entry to the body through a dog bite or dirty cut, since the germ lives in soil. After a variable interval fever and spasms begin to develop.

Tetanus is dangerous and requires intensive hospital treatment. Serum, containing antitoxin which neutralizes the poison, is of value if given early. See your doctor promptly after a dirty cut, especially injury from a garden fork.

Tetanus can be prevented by immunisation with a material called toxoid. In the UK this is routinely given to children as triple vaccine in the first year of life. Immunity following these jabs usually lasts for seven to eight years so periodic booster injections are given during the school years and are advised for those who work on the land, with animals or in 'dirty' occupations or if travelling to a Third World country. Hospital casualty departments give routine doses of tetanus toxoid to anyone attending with cuts and grazes. Patients are then recommended to complete the course by having two more injections at six weeks and six month intervals. They should take this advice seriously. Horse serum which used to be given and which caused many allergic reactions is no longer used in the UK.

Thermometer
(*See* TEMPERATURE.)

Thrombosis
The formation of a blood clot within a blood vessel. Normally this never occurs, but when a vessel is injured or diseased clotting sometimes takes place. Any part of the body may be the site of a thrombosis, and the symptoms will depend on the organ involved. If the clot is carried by the blood to some other site it is known as an embolus. Common danger sites for thrombosis are

in the coronary arteries (*see* HEART DISEASE) and the *deep* veins in the calf. (Thrombosis of the cerebral arteries tends to occur only in the old.)

There is a slightly increased risk of thrombosis for older women on the pill and a much increased risk if they smoke. Women waiting for a planned operation should give up the pill for six weeks before and stop smoking.

Thrombosis in the deep veins of the calf and thigh should not be confused with minor problems in superficial varicose veins (*see* VARICOSE VEINS). The former tends to occur after surgery or childbirth if there is prolonged immobilisation in bed. Stagnation of the blood in these veins can lead to thrombosis and the formation of emboli which travel to the lungs (*see* EMBOLISM). The leg is swollen and bending upwards of the foot is acutely painful. Nowadays the early mobilisation after surgery and childbirth prevents many of these complications.

The thrombosed vein usually gradually opens up and other blood channels enlarge so that any leg swelling slowly subsides. Tablets to reduce clotting are given for six to twelve weeks to prevent emboli. A supporting bandage is applied to the leg and the patient is mobilised as soon as possible. Whilst on anti-coagulant tablets the patient needs regular blood tests to check that the clotting factors are staying at the acceptable level. There are several different treatments which may be prescribed following a coronary thrombosis. Some research suggests an aspirin a day may prevent further attacks. As thrombosis interferes with the normal circulation to an organ, treatment aims at care for the damaged area until recovery, whilst preventing further clots. Urgent medical advice is always needed.

Thyrotoxicosis
Due to over-action of the thyroid gland. (*See* GOITRE.)

Tic

Spasmodic twitching of the face or eyelids. It may be hereditary or accompany disorders of the nervous system but generally it indicates stress. Cure depends on elimination of the causes of tension.

Tinea

Name of many fungus infections of the skin. Tinea cruris is commoner in men and causes inflamed itchy patches of skin in the groins and inner aspects of the thighs. Tinea pedis is another name for ATHLETE'S FOOT. Tinea capitis and Tinea corporis are other names for RINGWORM. These conditions are spread by the use of communal towels, bath mats, etc. These practices should be avoided as fungi thrive in slightly damp areas. Various creams are available from a pharmacy.

Tinnitus

A noise in the ears such as ringing, buzzing or roaring. Some noises in the ears may be due to a remediable cause such as catarrh, middle ear infection or wax when they will disappear on removal of the cause. A pulsating sound in the ear may occur with high blood pressure which can be treated. Tinnitus proper, disorder of the nerve of hearing, cannot be cured except occasionally where there is a removable nerve tumour; tablets may be prescribed to help. *True tinnitus always signifies some permanent hearing loss and is unfortunately becoming prevalent among youngsters in the pop scene due to prolonged exposure to loud noise.* When combined with giddiness and deafness the condition is known as Menière's disease. (*See* DEAFNESS, GIDDINESS.)

Tongue

Inspection of the tongue is not the ritual it was as there are likely to be other important areas to be examined. Generally, in the healthy non-smoker it is clean and moist and covered in small raised areas – the papillae.

'Invisible' tastebuds are widespread over the tongue and soft palate. If you are feeling well, do not look at your tongue for signs of blemishes. A small coating (brown in smokers) can appear in the healthiest now and then. The tongue will tend to be furred in any feverish condition. Antibiotics may cause a 'dark' tongue due to fungus infection which can be cleared by anti-fungus lozenges. Persistent furring can sometimes be removed by fresh pineapple juice. Brushing with a soft toothbrush helps. A smooth, sore tongue can be a sign of anaemia and the tongue can be the site of infection, ulcer or tumour.

Tonsillitis

The tonsils are two small tissues on either side of the back of the throat *(see Fig. 13)*. They are part of the lymphatic gland system (*see* GLANDS), and trap germs which enter through the mouth. Naturally they are frequently attacked themselves, the resulting inflammation being *tonsillitis*. The first symptom is a sore

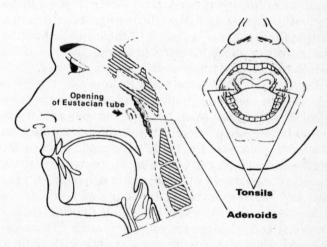

Fig. 13 Tonsils and adenoids

throat, and if this is examined it will be seen to be inflamed. The temperature rises, the patient feels unwell, and often has a headache. As the condition progresses, the tonsils become swollen; and often can be seen to have little beads of pus (white spots) on them. The patient should see a doctor promptly as he may need pencillin. Recurrent attacks of tonsillitis and persistently enlarged neck glands suggest that the tonsils are no longer working and may be best removed. (*See* ADENOIDS.)

Toothache

Usually due to decay which causes a cavity in a tooth or an abscess around it. See your dentist without delay; but sometimes delay is unavoidable and temporary relief required. It is difficult to suppress toothache, but one of the following may help. Soluble aspirin taken in a little water may help. The mouth should be rinsed with water, as hot as one can bear and this swilled around the aching area. Alcohol can bring relief. A piece of cotton wool soaked in neat whisky can be applied to the tooth. Clove oil is often effective, and used in the same way. A pinch of table salt laid on the tooth is worth trying. Avoid cold food or drink. Do not bite on the affected tooth until it has been treated.

Tooth decay is due to many factors but the most important is diet. The frequency of eating sugary food is more important than the amount eaten. Sweets should not be eaten between meals. If eaten at the end of a meal make sure the teeth are cleaned afterwards. Teeth should be cleaned twice a day, preferably with a flouride-containing toothpaste. If you live in an area with low fluoride levels in the tap water, children's teeth can be strengthened by giving fluoride tablets (from chemist's) during the years of growth. Habits are acquired when young so make sure children use their own toothbrushes. A six monthly check with your dentist is essential to catch any possible trouble early.

Meanwhile, the use of dental floss helps to remove dental plaque (where the rot starts).

Torsion of Testis

The twisting of a testicle on its stalk leading to strangulation of the blood supply and risk of severe tissue damage if not restored rapidly to a normal position. The signs may resemble orchitis, i.e. swelling and acute pain; often vomiting occurs. Any male (often a boy) with these symptoms needs urgent medical assessment as a small operation is needed as soon as possible to prevent degeneration of the testicle. (*See* ORCHITIS.)

Toxin

Medical name for a poison produced by a germ. The toxins of diphtheria and tetanus are responsible for all the symptoms of the diseases. When invaded by germs the body can produce an *anti-toxin* which will neutralize the toxin. The basis of serum treatment, used in a number of diseases, is to supply the correct anti-toxin artificially.

Toxoplasmosis

A disease found all over the world and transmitted to humans by cats and dogs as well as other domestic animals. In adults it causes a sore throat and glandular swellings. Its real danger lies in the fact that it can be transmitted to the unborn child in which it can cause mental defects and/or blindness.

Train Sickness (*See* TRAVEL SICKNESS.)

Transplants

Transplantation surgery is a modern technique by which certain organs can be transferred to patients with severely diseased ones. With kidneys, a living donor, usually a close relative with 'matching' tissue can be used, and the operations to remove one kidney from the donor and transfer it to the patient are performed simultaneously. In the case of liver, heart and in other kidney transplantations the organs of fatal accident victims are usually used. This is because at the time of death the organs are generally not affected by disease. An exception is the cornea (transparent membrane at the front of the eye). It is often of value at whatever age the donor died.

Apart from the cornea, which can restore sight to those afflicted with a disease causing clouding in this transparent membrane, the most successful transplants are kidney. Many thousands of people are alive and well because of a kidney transplant. They usually feel fitter than when dependent on a kidney machine. To prevent the body rejecting the 'foreign' organ, special drugs need to be taken. There is always a shortage of suitable donor kidneys. Kidney donor cards available from doctors' surgeries, health clinics and hospitals should be carried by anyone who wishes his kidneys to be used for transplant after his death. People who wish to donate their eyes (corneas) after death should contact the Secretary General of the Royal National Institute for the Blind for details. Heart and lung as well as liver transplants are increasingly taking place in special centres and are saving lives.

Travel Sickness

The ear is an organ of balance as well as of hearing (*see* GIDDINESS). When the balancing mechanism is over-stimulated it may set up a reflex (*see* PAIN) within the brain which causes vomiting. This is the basis of travel sickness which is due to constant motion, and the mechanism is the same whether it be sea, air (*see* EARACHE), car or train sickness. Some people are better able to stand movement than others; but in everyone the balancing mechanism can gradually adjust itself, so that after some days the tendency to sickness wears off.

The worst time is at the beginning of a journey, and it is then that precautions are most required.

It is best not to load the stomach, and only a light meal should be taken before embarking by those who are prone to sickness. Tablets which can be obtained at the chemists may help. Looking down seems to upset the vomiting reflex so reading, especially in a car, is not advisable. Taking an interest in the surrounding scenery and having an occasional barley sugar sweet is beneficial. (*See* VOMITING.)

Tremor *(Shaking)*
Means involuntary shaking of hands or other parts due to some imbalance of the muscle and nerve action. Some people are born with naturally rather unsteady hands and this is generally of no significance. Most people become rather tremulous when nervous and again this is the normal response to fear. With increasing age it is usual for the hands to be less steady than in youth.

If tremor is of fairly sudden onset, is present at all times without obvious reason, or is causing accidents, see a doctor as it could be a symptom of remediable illnesses such as thyrotoxicosis (*see* GOITRE).

Tuberculosis
Is caused by a specific germ – the tubercle bacillus. It lives within a special protecting membrane, and is difficult to kill, so that the infection is usually long and drawn out. Any part of the body may be attacked, but the common site is in the lungs, *pulmonary tuberculosis*. Germs are spread by persons who have the disease, and after being breathed in, they settle in the lung and multiply. Tuberculosis causes a breaking down of the normal lung tissue, so that cavities may form.

Occasionally the disease may occur in other sites such as bones, kidney and Fallopian tubes. However, it responds to modern anti-tuberculous antibiotics. Hospital admission is seldom necessary. Anti-tuberculous drugs need to be taken for many months but the patient can be at home whilst taking them.

The relative infrequency of the disease in the UK is predominately due to public health measures, mass X-ray screening, improved nutrition, housing and effective drugs. There is also a vaccine called BCG which is usually given to school children at thirteen after a skin test (Mantoux). If the skin test is negative this means that the child is not immune to tuberculosis and the vaccine is given. A positive skin test usually means that the child has met the tubercle germ already but fought it off. A chest X-ray is arranged to check that there is no disease. When tuberculosis was common this type of 'natural' immunity was frequent.

There has been a recent slight increase in the incidence of tuberculosis in the UK, especially in areas with large Asian populations and in the elderly. Anyone with a cough persisting for more than three weeks should go to their doctor. It is of course still extremely common in Third World countries.

Tumour
A swelling. People become alarmed if they hear of a tumour, since tumours are a common symptom of cancer. The word simply means 'lump', and many tumours are unrelated to cancer.

Typhoid Fever (*Enteric Fever*)
An infection of the intestines with the typhoid group of germs. Symptoms are similar to dysentery (*see* DYSENTERY), although CONSTIPATION may be an early symptom along with fever, before a rash, abdominal pain and diarrhoea appear. The disease is more serious than dysentery but responds well to antibiotics like chloramphenicol, ampicillin or ciproxin. Immunisation protects to a large degree against typhoid and should be given to those travelling outside Northern Europe, Northern

America, Australia or New Zealand. The disease is spread by contaminated water and food and has been virtually eliminated in the UK by public health measures.

Typhus Fevers
A group of diseases caused by a micro-organism (Rickettsia). It is transmitted to humans by mites, lice, fleas or ticks, often passed on from other animals such as sheep or deer. One such disease in the UK is known as 'Q' fever in which skin rashes and a form of pneumonia occur.

U

Ulcer

The breaking down of skin or membrane to form an open sore which may become inflamed or infected. Treatment depends on the type. Recurrent small ulcers in the mouth can be helped by putting Corlan pellets on them, or Bioral gel. (*See* DUODENAL ULCER, GASTRIC ULCER, VARICOSE VEINS, X-RAYS.)

Ultrasound

A form of radiant energy now routinely used in pregnancy to determine the maturity or size of the unborn baby without usually potentially harmful X-rays.

It is also used extensively in hospital centres to diagnose diseases of the liver, kidney and other organs. It is also used in the treatment of painful muscular or ligament disorders along with other forms of physio-therapy, heat, massage, etc.

Ultraviolet

A form of radiant energy beyond the violet end of the spectrum; it is useful in skin disorders such as acne and psoriasis. As part of natural solar energy it enables the skin to produce its own natural vitamin D – responsible for strong bones and teeth.

Undescended Testicle

The testicle normally lies within the abdominal cavity before birth. By the time the baby is born it should have moved down to occupy its position within a special sac of skin, the scrotum. Sometimes one or both organs fail to do this, and the condition is then known as an undescended testicle. Unless it occupies its normal position it cannot function properly. Sometimes it can be made to descend by means of hormone injections, but often a small operation is necessary. Remember that in small boys the testicles can retract up out of the scrotum – especially if examined with cold hands! Parents can check that the scrotum contains two small oval firm lumps at bathtime when everything is warm. Some specialists like to treat youngsters with undescended testicles at the age of four or five (others prefer to wait longer to see if natural descent will occur). If parents suspects this condition in their four-year-old they should see their doctor.

Uraemia
It occurs when the kidneys are no longer capable of filtering the poisonous waste products from the blood. There are many treatments for kidney failure ranging from low protein diet to artificial kidney machines and, of course, kidney transplants.

Urticaria
(*See* NETTLERASH.)

Uterus (*Womb*)
(*See* BIRTH *and* CERVIX.)

V

Vaccination
Procedure used to protect against SMALLPOX by introducing germs called vaccinia into the body – now generally applied to all IMMUNISATION.

Vagina
The female passage. Its entrance lies between the bladder and bowel outlets. The opening is flanked by the two pairs of skin folds known as the labia majora and minora. The labia minora meet some way in front of the vaginal entrance and partially cover the sensitive clitoris.

Vaginitis (*Leucorrhoea*)
Inflammation of the vagina causing itching, soreness, painful intercourse and discharge which may be blood stained. This can occur in the absence of infection after the menopause when it is due to the lining becoming thinner and less resilient as oestrogen levels decline. This type of vaginitis may be helped by oestrogen cream but your doctor's advice is essential first. This vaginitis may go on to become infected by germs and may be associated with troublesome cystitis (*see* CYSTITIS). Treatment may be by pessaries or oval tablets depending on the type of germ.

Vaginal infection can of course occur at any time of life and a variety of germs like monilia (thrush) and trichomonas (TV) as well as those of sexually transmitted disease may be the cause. Your family doctor can help with all of these infections although if you have risked sexually transmitted infection by casual sexual contact it is probably wise to go straight to a special clinic. A discharge due to vaginitis can generally be distinguished from normal secretion by associated irritation or odour. A common cause of very offensive discharge is a retained tampon. Little girls are prone to vaginitis for, like their grannies, they too have low oestrogen levels. Persistent soreness and discharge in a child needs medical advice as apart from other considerations it may be due to the introduction of a 'foreign body' such as a bead. Threadworms are another possible cause.

Varicocele (*See also* VARICOSE VEINS.)
Name of a collection of dilated blood vessels in the scrotum – similar to varicose veins, and usually not serious. Sometimes a varicocele will cause aching and discomfort, when it can be removed by a small operation, or a suspensary bandage will sometimes meet the case. The condition may largely improve by the age of 30 when the bandage can be discarded.

A varicocele which may be associated with infertility can be treated by operation; it is safe and most men would prefer this to a bandage.

Varicose Veins
Blood which circulates to the legs returns to the heart in thin-walled vessels. Some of these vessels, or veins, run just beneath the skin, and contain valves which prevent the blood from running down again into the leg. These surface veins connect with the deep veins in the leg by veins known as perforators.

In adults, the valves in the surface and perforating veins may become weakened, and the walls of the veins have to bear increased pressure. In consequence the veins become swollen and twisted, i.e. *varicose*. If the condition is left untreated the nourishment of the skin by fresh blood is interfered with, and an ulcer may occur (a *varicose ulcer*) which can be difficult to heal.

Some varicose veins can be treated by injection, which is simple. The swollen veins are emptied of blood by elevating the leg, and it is firmly bandaged afterwards and the patient is advised to walk at least three miles a day. This is to encourage blood flow in the more important *deep* veins which are in the muscles of the leg. The bandage can usually be discarded after about six weeks but it is good to continue the walking exercises and avoid standing for long periods. The small injection causes the vein to shrivel and disappear.

Some varicose veins can be controlled by supporting stockings or tights but these must be put on first thing in the morning before rising (i.e. before the surface veins become engorged by gravity). They must also extend well above the site of the highest varicose vein. It is no good wearing a knee length stocking when there are varicose veins in the thigh; this can make matters worse. An operation may be required to tie off or remove the vein. If a varicose ulcer has developed, it is essential that these veins should receive treatment – perhaps removal of associated veins; in addition the leg will need special dressings and compression bandaging while the ulcer heals. Your doctor can arrange for the community nurse to do this. The earlier that treatment for varicose veins can be started the better. One aims to avoid complications and persistent leg pain. Varicose veins commonly occur during pregnancy and the best treatment is to wear supporting maternity tights and keep the feet up as much as possible. They usually recede quite a bit after the pregnancy is over.

Vasectomy
(*See* CONTRACEPTION.)

Venereal Disease *(VD)*
(*See* GONORRHOEA, SYPHILIS, NSU *and* SEXUALLY TRANS-MITTED DISEASES.)

Verruca
(*See* WART.)

Vertigo
A sensation of movement of the surroundings; this can be rotational or horizontal and vertical. It is due to some temporary disturbance of the inner ear perhaps infection or upset in circulation. Tablets are often helpful. A combination of tinnitus, vertigo and hearing loss is known as Menière's disease. Treatment is by tablets or occasionally by operation. (*See* GIDDINESS.)

Virus
Many germs which cause disease in man can be seen under a powerful light microscope. In one group the germs are so tiny that they cannot be seen except under the modern electron microscope. These are known as viruses and unfortunately there is very little specific treatment for virus infections. Virus infections tend to be complicated by bacterial infections at a later stage so that antibiotics may help to treat and prevent complications.

Vitamin
(*See article on page 11.*)

Vomiting (*Sickness*)
Vomiting is brought about by contraction of the stomach muscles which empties the stomach of its contents. The commonest cause is irritation by unsuitable or excessive food. Vomiting helps to protect the body from the unpleasant effects that might follow if the offending material were not eliminated. Examples are the eating of green apples by children, or excess alcohol by adults. Germs and food poison result in vomiting, and sometimes it is associated with disease of the stomach or intestines, for example GASTRIC or DUODENAL ULCER. Vomiting is controlled by a part of

the brain, and if this becomes irritated sickness may occur without the stomach itself being irritated. This type is seen in MIGRAINE and in a variety of feverish illnesses. The vomiting in TRAVEL SICKNESS is also due to reflex irritation of the 'vomiting centre'. Vomiting also can be due to psychological reasons.

In the treatment of vomiting remember children tend to vomit more readily than adults and often get rid of phlegm in this way. If there is an obvious cause (e.g. too rich food and drink) the sickness will pass and need not alarm. Vomiting which occurs for no apparent reason or persists or is accompanied by pain should receive medical advice. 'Coffee ground' appearance of the vomited material may indicate blood requiring urgent medical attention. (*See* HAEMATEMESIS.)

W

Wart *(Verruca)*

Small, hard outgrowths from the skin. They usually occur on hands and feet, are mildly contagious, and may spread on the same person, or to another. Caused by a virus, warts sometimes disappear after months or years but because of the danger of spreading are best treated. Warts on the sole of the foot become compressed and painful and are usually known by their 'correct' name of verrucae. They can be cured by chemicals but it can be time consuming. People with verrucae are excluded from public swimming pools and should not take part in communal barefoot activities. Chiropodists will treat verrucae and there are Verruca Clinics. Stubborn verrucae can be frozen with carbon dioxide 'snow' in hospital out-patients' clinics (a doctor's letter is necessary).

Wax

Soft wax is normally produced in the canal which leads to the ear drum. Some people produce more than others and if wax accumulates it becomes dry and hard and may reduce hearing or irritate. It can be removed by a doctor or nurse by syringing with warm water: it helps if the patient uses some softening drops for a few days before the syringing. It is folly to try to remove the wax by syringing or poking things into the ear yourself, since the delicate ear drum may be damaged.

Wen

(See CYST.)

White Leg

Popular name for a condition which sometimes occurs in women after confinement. Fortunately it is rare due to the practice of encouraging women to get up and about as soon as reasonably possible after the birth. It is due to a blood clot in the circulation of the leg (*see* THROMBOSIS), and the limb becomes white, swollen and often painful. The condition needs urgent medical attention as the blood clot may dislodge from the leg and come to rest in the lung (*see* EMBOLISM). Special drugs can be given to diminish clotting and may be continued for six to twelve weeks. Blood tests at weekly intervals are needed to monitor the degree of 'blood thinning'.

Whitlow

Infection in the fold of tissue on either side of the fingernail – it can spread below the nail. Bathing in hot salt water may bring the infection to a head and allow pus to escape. If infection persists and spreads below the nail, antibiotics and perhaps drainage of pus may be necessary. (*See* FINGER, SEPTIC.)

Whooping Cough

A specific infectious illness, usually in children, caused by a bacillus. The disease often occurs in epidemics and may be grave in babies. A second attack is unusual, but older children or adults, who have escaped infection, sometimes catch the disease. The germs are spread through the air, and the incubation period (*see* QUARANTINE) is usually about a fortnight. Early symptoms resemble those of a 'cold', but continue longer with an increasing cough. The characteristic 'whoops' do not usually develop for about two to three weeks. There is severe coughing which the child is unable to control; the face may become blue, and finally the breath is drawn in with a 'whoop'. These attacks occur a variable number of times a day, depending on the severity of infection, and are often troublesome at night. They are frequently followed by vomiting. This acute stage lasts from one to three weeks and antibiotics such as erythromycin are usually prescribed. Intensive care in hospital may be necessary in treating the very young who may develop complications such as pneumonia.

Advice should be sought at the first signs of spasmodic cough in a child in case it may be whooping cough. The child is rested during the feverish stage of the illness but may be allowed up when he is feeling better and more lively. If a child wants to be up and about he is usually well enough to do so. He should not return to school or playgroup until at least three weeks after the cough started – assuming he feels well and energetic. He should have a final check from the doctor to make sure that the chest is clear before returning to school and at least a week of convalescence including outdoor walks to make sure that cold air does not provoke more coughing spasms. A minor degree of cough may persist for weeks, but provided the child is otherwise well and lively it can be ignored.

Immunisation is offered free to babies, in the form of 'Triple' vaccine (it also contains protection against diphtheria and tetanus) at three, five and eleven months. Whooping cough is serious and can permanently damage the lungs and brain in severe cases. There has recently been anxiety about occasional harmful effects of the vaccine in causing brain damage. Epidemics of whooping cough cause much more damage than the vaccine but if you are worried about triple vaccine discuss this with your doctor. An alternative vaccine containing only the diphtheria and tetanus components can be given instead.

Womb
(*See* BIRTH *and* CERVIX.)

Worms

Various worms can inhabit the body. Their eggs are usually eaten accidentally with food and hatch in the digestive tract where they live on their host's food. Small worm infestation seldom causes serious symptoms; but *roundworms* and *tapeworms* can take a considerable proportion of the nourishment and may disturb general health, and cause such side effects as anaemia or loss of weight. One of the common worms in the UK is the *threadworm*, which usually affects children. It appears in the stools from time to time, where it resembles short pieces of white thread. If suspicious watch for it. It may cause itching, particularly at night, since the worms come out onto the buttocks to lay their eggs. This irritation may be a cause of bedwetting and in girls scratching can lead to secondary infection and vaginal discharge.

Threadworms can be cured easily by appropriate medicines, such as Antepar and Pripsen, but reinfection must be guarded against. If itchy, children will tend to scratch their buttocks at night so thumb suckers and nail biters are particularly at risk from reinfection. Nails should be cut short and scrupulous hygiene observed. Everyone should have their own face cloths and towel which should be boiled after use. If one member of a family has threadworms treat the whole family. Other types of worm may infest man, but they are not common in the UK. Any persistent itching round the buttocks or the appearance of worms in the stools should be reported to your doctor.

Hookworm (*see* HOOKWORM) is commonly seen in people who have lived in Africa and can cause problems in the bladder with bleeding. Other worms seen in Asians and Africans living in the UK are *filaria* (*see* FILARIASIS), which cause eye and circulation problems.

X

X-Rays

Invisible to the eye, they resemble light rays in many ways but have greater penetration. Just as light will pass through glass, X-rays pass through the tissues of the body. In common with light rays, X-rays can change a photographic plate, which property makes them useful in medicine. By shining X-rays through a part of the body we can photograph the shadows they cast, and X-ray photographs reveal a number of internal disorders such as bone fractures which cannot otherwise be seen. The internal structure of the stomach and intestines can be studied by giving the patient an opaque substance such as barium sulphate to swallow (it can also be given as an enema into the lower bowels). The barium fills all the cavities and crevices of the intestines showing up ulcers or tumours. Another substance is given when the gall bladder is to be studied. A radio-opaque dye can be injected into the blood and photographed as it is filtered through the kidneys. This outlines the kidneys and bladder, demonstrates damage, stones or tumours and to some extent indicates the efficiency of the organ in filtering. Apart from the discovery of disease, or diagnosis, X-rays are useful in treating a number of conditions. In large doses the rays damage, and may kill cells, and this may be very useful in some cancers or in certain blood diseases.

Index

References in CAPITALS are emergency ones, also shown on page 6. References in **bold type** are ones which are also main articles in the encyclopedia.

281

Urethra, 82, 201
Urethritis, 201
Uric acid, 129
Urination, frequency of, 120
Urine, retention of, 223–224
Urticaria, 187

V
Vaccination, 145–146, 155, 173, 252, 260, **264,** 271
Vagina, 79, 229, **264**
Vaginitis, 264–265
Vagotomy, 99
Varicocele, 265
Varicose veins, 77, 176, 204, **265–266**
Vasectomy, 81
Vegetarian diet, 13
Veins, 37, 204, 265–266
Vena cava, 136
Venereal diseases, 127–128, 152, 188–189, 194, 233–234, 246–250
Ventricle, 135
Verruca, 269
Vertigo, 267
Vesicles, 221

Viral meningitis, 175
Virus, 267
Vitamins, 11, 226–227, 232, 238
Vomiting, 77, 192, **267–268**

W
Wart, 269
Wasp stings, 242
Waters, breaking of the, 49
Wax, 103, 254, **269**
Weight, 12, 142, 175, 191–192, 193
Weil's disease, 164
Wen, 86
White leg, 270
Whitlow, 270
Whooping cough, 61, 220, **270–271**
Windpipe, 136
Womb, 79, 103–104, 143, 213–214, 224, 229
Worms, 272
Wrist sprain, 240

X
X-rays, 273

Mediawatch

14 SEP 1995   Checked 8/9/11
Was ref

17/12/15

Please renew/return items by last date
shown. Please call the number below:

Renewals and enquiries: 0300 123 4049

Textphone for hearing or
speech impaired users: 0300 123 4041

www.hertsdirect.org/librarycatalogue
L32

FA

To Keith,
who saw me through

Cassell
Wellington House
125 Strand
London WC2R 0BB

387 Park Avenue South
New York, NY 10016–8810

First published 1995

British Library Cataloguing-in-Publication Data
A catalogue record for this book is available from the British Library.

ISBN 0-304-331864

Typeset by York House Typographic Ltd, London W13 8NT
Printed and bound in Great Britain by Mackay's of Chatham plc